Trauma Studies and Literature

ANGLO-AMERIKANISCHE STUDIEN
ANGLO-AMERICAN STUDIES

Herausgegeben von Rüdiger Ahrens und Kevin Cope

Band 34

PETER LANG
Frankfurt am Main · Berlin · Bern · Bruxelles · New York · Oxford · Wien

Valentina Adami

Trauma Studies and Literature
Martin Amis's *Time's Arrow*
As Trauma Fiction

PETER LANG
Internationaler Verlag der Wissenschaften

Bibliographic Information published by the Deutsche Nationalbibliothek
The Deutsche Nationalbibliothek lists this publication in the Deutsche Nationalbibliografie; detailed bibliographic data is available in the internet at <http://www.d-nb.de>.

ISSN 0177-6959
ISBN 978-3-631-57796-7

© Peter Lang GmbH
Internationaler Verlag der Wissenschaften
Frankfurt am Main 2008
All rights reserved.

All parts of this publication are protected by copyright. Any utilisation outside the strict limits of the copyright law, without the permission of the publisher, is forbidden and liable to prosecution. This applies in particular to reproductions, translations, microfilming, and storage and processing in electronic retrieval systems.

Printed in Germany 1 2 3 4 5   7

www.peterlang.de

TABLE OF CONTENTS

INTRODUCTION 3

1. AN INTERDISCIPLINARY THEORETICAL APPROACH TO THE STUDY OF TRAUMA
   1.1 A brief history of the studies on trauma 9
   1.2 The social dimension of trauma 16
   1.3 Trauma and memory 26
   1.4 Trauma and testimony 31
   1.5 Trauma and history 37
   1.6 Representing the Holocaust 41
   1.7 Trauma as a pathology of history 46

2. MARTIN AMIS'S *TIME'S ARROW* AS TRAUMA FICTION
   2.1 Some preliminary considerations on art, ethics and language 49
   2.2 Martin Amis 59
   2.3 *Time's Arrow*: an introduction 60
   2.4 Intertextuality: Robert Jay Lifton's *The Nazi Doctors* 63
   2.5 The Holocaust between modernism and postmodernism 71
   2.6 What is trauma fiction? 73
   2.7 The significance of the time's reversal in *Time's Arrow* 77
   2.8 The status of the narrator in *Time's Arrow* 87
   2.9 The role of the reader in *Time's Arrow* 91

CONCLUSION: "STYLE *IS* MORALITY" 97

BIBLIOGRAPHY 103

INTRODUCTION

The Greek word *trauma* ("wound") originally referred to a physical injury. However, nowadays *trauma* also refers to a wound of the spirit, that is, an injury inflicted upon the mind. In psychology and psychiatry, the existence of a posttraumatic syndrome was first officially recognized in 1980, in the third edition of the *Diagnostic and Statistical Manual of Mental Disorders (DSM III)*, where the term Post-Traumatic Stress Disorder (PTSD) was adopted for the first time. Since then, the official clinical definition of PTSD has been revised and updated by the American Psychiatric Association (APA) in the subsequent editions of the *Diagnostic and Statistical Manual*.

According to the current edition of the *DSM*, an event can be considered as traumatic if it "involved actual or threatened death or serious injury, or a threat to the physical integrity of self or others", and if it is "persistently reexperienced in [...] recurrent and intrusive distressing recollections"[1]. In fact, trauma causes the individual's mind to hold on to the moment of the traumatic event, "preventing it from slipping back into its proper chronological place in the past"[2], so that the individual relives the event over and over again in compulsive repetitions: "[t]he moment becomes a season, the event becomes a condition"[3].

However, the study of trauma does not only raise clinical issues, but also cultural ones, because the experience of trauma is a culturally and socially embedded phenomenon: according to sociologist Kai Erikson, trauma is "a concept social scientists as well as clinicians can work with"[4]. In fact, trauma can affect not only individuals, but also societies and cultures, so that it is possible to distinguish between *individual trauma*, which impinges on the psyche of the individual, and *collective trauma*, which affects society as a whole and, as we will see in chapter two, has the power to shape cultural identities.

Erikson underlines the difference between individual and collective trauma as follows:

> By individual trauma I mean a blow to the psyche that breaks through one's defenses so suddenly and with such brutal force that one cannot react to it effectively. [...]
> By collective trauma, on the other hand, I mean a blow to the basic tissues of social life that damages the bonds attaching people together

---

[1] American Psychiatric Association, *Diagnostic and Statistical Manual of Mental Disorders DSM-IV-TR (Text Revision)*, 4th ed. rev., Washington: American Psychiatric Publishing, 2000, p. 463.
[2] K. Erikson, "Notes on Trauma and Community", in C. Caruth, ed., *Trauma: Explorations in Memory*, Baltimore: Johns Hopkins University Press, 1995, p. 185.
[3] *Ibid.*
[4] *Ibid.*

and impairs the prevailing sense of communality. The collective trauma works its way slowly and insidiously into the awareness of those who suffer from it, so it does not have the quality of suddenness normally associated with "trauma". But it is a form of shock all the same, a gradual realization that the community no longer exists as an effective source of support and that an important part of the self has disappeared.[5]

Since the 1990s, the study of trauma has become a major concern for literary and cultural critics, insofar as it is related to social, historical, literary and cultural phenomena: "trauma is also psychocultural, because *the injury entails the interpretation of the injury*"[6]. Since interpretations of trauma are influenced by the cultural context, trauma and culture are inextricably linked:

> A culture may make terror and loss heroically meaningful and so diminish its damage, but a culture may also contribute to psychic ruin. For exactly this reason – because trauma can be ideologically manipulated, reinforced, and exploited – it calls for critical analysis as well as psychiatric intervention.[7]

Words and trauma have a reciprocal influence. Therefore, the main concern of Trauma Studies in literature is analysing the effects of trauma on words, and the way words deal with trauma: "[I]ts main focus is on words that wound, and presumably can be healed, if at all, by further words"[8]. The study of trauma is thus relevant to literary and cultural criticism, because it helps us "'read the wound' with the aid of literature"[9] and acknowledge the relation between "psychic wounds and signification"[10].

Moreover, the study of trauma through literary texts can provide us with "a clearer view of the relation of literature to mental functioning in several key areas, including reference, subjectivity, and narration"[11]. Hartman further emphasizes the importance of trauma theory for the study of literature by claiming:

---

[5] K. Erikson, *Everything in Its Path*, New York: Simon and Schuster, 1976, pp. 153-4.
[6] K. Farrell, *Post-traumatic Culture. Injury and Interpretation in the Nineties*, Baltimore, London: Johns Hopkins University Press, 1998, p. 7.
[7] Ibid.
[8] G. Hartman, "Trauma Within the Limits of Literature", *European Journal of English Studies (EJES)* 7.3 (2003), pp. 57-9.
[9] G. Hartman, "On Traumatic Knowledge and Literary Studies", *New Literary History: A Journal of Theory and Interpretation* 26.3 (1995), p. 537.
[10] G. Hartman, "Trauma Within the Limits of Literature", p. 59.
[11] G. Hartman, "On Traumatic Knowledge", p. 542.

Not that trauma theory, at least when it works within the orbit of literary studies, has definitive answers. But instead of seeking premature knowledge, it stays longer in the negative and allows disturbances of language and mind the quality of time we give to literature.[12]

The study of trauma is a cross-disciplinary issue that challenges traditional modes of understanding and blurs traditional disciplinary boundaries. In fact, trauma disrupts genres and collapses distinctions, promoting an interaction among different disciplinary areas: no single discipline "owns" trauma as a subject matter. Hence, the approach of Trauma Studies to literature takes into account the multifaceted perspectives of literature, history, psychoanalysis, sociology, anthropology, psychiatry, and neurobiology.

The interdisciplinary perspective of Trauma Studies requires collaboration among scholars of the different fields, and a flexible approach that not only recognizes the mutual relevance of the various disciplines in shaping knowledge, but also respects their histories, assumptions and frameworks of interpretation. Unfortunately, as Hartman points out, the tensions among scholars of the different disciplines have undermined the attempts to join the various areas of study in the humanities: in particular, as historians reject the idea that history writing is subject to linguistic and literary structures, that is, to tropes and plots, literary theorists refuse the historians' claim that objectivity and truthfulness are possible[13].

However, according to literary critic and trauma theorist Cathy Caruth, trauma favours a translation between disciplines and areas of culture precisely because it overwhelms the self and disorients society, thus questioning the very limits of our understanding:

> The more we satisfactorily locate and classify the symptoms of PTSD, the more we seem to have dislocated the boundaries of our modes of understanding – so that psychoanalysis and medically oriented psychiatry, sociology, history and even literature all seem to be called upon to explain, to cure, or to show why it is that we can no longer simply explain or simply cure. The phenomenon of trauma has seemed to become all-inclusive, but it has done so precisely because it brings us to the limits of our understanding: if psychoanalysis, psychiatry, sociology, and even literature are beginning to hear each other anew in the study of trauma, it is because they are listening through the radical disruption and gaps of traumatic experience.[14]

---

[12] *Ibid.*
[13] G. Hartman, *Scars of the Spirit: The Struggle Against Inauthenticity,* New York: Palgrave MacMillan, 2002, p. 224.
[14] C. Caruth, "Trauma and Experience: Introduction", in C. Caruth (ed.), *Trauma: Explorations in memory*, Baltimore: Johns Hopkins University Press, 1995, pp. 3-4.

Traumatic events disrupt the victim's mental schemes and cause a disjunction between experiencing, understanding and verbalizing, because the experience of trauma cannot be integrated into prior frameworks of knowledge. Trauma Studies thus urges us to rethink the ethical and epistemological categories according to which we perceive and analyse reality, questioning the possibility of objective and certain knowledge, and suggesting the existence of a traumatic kind of knowledge "that cannot be made entirely conscious, in the sense of being fully retrieved or communicated without distortion"[15].

The disruptions caused by trauma, and by the Holocaust in particular, pose challenges and open up possibilities within contemporary thought, making possible new insights in the disciplines involved in its study. According to historian Dominick LaCapra,

> [t]he centrality of the Holocaust in Western consciousness is related to the kind of challenge it poses to certain forms of Western self-understanding. If we really believe that the West is the high point of civilization [...], and if we really do see the story of the West as that of enlightenment, then it's very difficult to come to terms with the Holocaust within that frame of reference.[16]

This could explain the increase of interest in trauma in our era, characterized, as Kirby Farrell underlines, by a "post-traumatic culture"[17].

Trauma Studies have inherited from Holocaust Studies the idea of the unrepresentability and unspeakability of trauma. However, although the Holocaust is indeed the crucial concern of Trauma Studies, trauma is a broader issue that includes other traumatic events, ranging from individual and private traumas such as rape, abortion, or illness, to collective traumas such as wars, genocides, or natural disasters. The ethical inclination of Trauma Studies invites us to move beyond the rhetoric of the sublime singularity and uniqueness of the Holocaust, in order to allow comparisons and forge links among different historical traumas.

LaCapra argues that the overemphasis on the Holocaust in the popular culture and the politics of America might represent a denial of the traumas with which America is directly involved, such as that of the African Americans and the Native Americans: emphasizing the traumas of others in the past might be a way of not looking at contemporary, more pressing traumas[18]. Of course, he does not mean that the Holocaust is not a significant problem: "if you are trying to

---

[15] G. Hartman, "On Traumatic Knowledge and Literary Studies", p. 537.
[16] D. LaCapra, *Writing History, Writing Trauma*, Baltimore: Johns Hopkins University Press, 2000, p. 176.
[17] K. Farrell, *Post-traumatic Culture*, p. 2.
[18] D. LaCapra, *Writing*, p. 171.

understand the twentieth century and Western history in general", and, I would add, the experience of trauma as well, "the Holocaust is a problem with which you, to some extent, have to be concerned in an informed way"[19].

In our postmodern and post-Holocaust era, disorder is an integral part of life, meaning and coherence are systematically undermined, and reality is unstable. Recognizing the analogies between the postmodern condition, the structure of traumatic experiences, and that of literary texts may help us clarify the symbolic processes of signification that organize knowledge both in the individual's mind and in literary texts. Thus, the study of trauma can provide a fruitful insight not only into the human psyche but also into contemporary literature, society and culture.

Moreover, literature can offer a different perspective for approaching trauma: in a context characterized by a constant repetition of scenes of violence in the media, which risks domesticating the impact of trauma, literature has the power to engage the reader with the traumatic narrative, and to avoid the "desensitization" caused by the transformation of trauma into cliché. In fact, trauma fiction usually overlaps with postmodern fiction in its refusal of closure and coherence, proposing disruptive forms of narrative that depart from conventional plot structures.

Traumatic literature aims at bearing witness to trauma by representing it as something disturbing that has not been fully apprehended. Therefore, it adopts techniques which mirror the effects of trauma, following the assumption that the impact of trauma can only be represented by mimicking its symptoms through a self-conscious use of style. In particular, through a disrupted chronology and a fragmented narrative voice, trauma fiction aims at reproducing the collapse of temporality and the crisis of truth that characterize traumatic experiences.

The focus of the present study is Martin Amis's novel *Time's Arrow*[20], which I consider as one of the most seminal examples of trauma fiction. The breakdown of chronology, coherence and predictability in this novel resembles the breakdown of meaning caused by trauma in the individual's mind. Amis's novel represents a powerful – and, I think, successful – attempt to avoid desensitization by reproducing the shocking force of trauma through a shocking narrative form: the life of a Nazi doctor is narrated backwards, from death to birth, so that the reader cannot understand who the protagonist really is until half way through the book.

The strategy of the time's reversal deprives us of our ease of reading, thus forcing us to be more active and attentive, and to reflect on the immense horror

---

[19] *Ibid.*, p. 172.
[20] M. Amis, *Time's Arrow, or the Nature of the Offence*, London: Penguin Books, 1992. [First published by Jonathan Cape, 1991]. All subsequent references to the Penguin edition are given in brackets within the body of the text.

of the Holocaust. Moreover, the reader is actively involved in creating meaning because the criticism against the crimes perpetrated by the Nazis is not explicit, not overtly expressed in the narrator's words. Hence, by representing trauma in the disruptive forms of traumatic literature, *Time's Arrow* prevents indifference and favours an empathetic and ethically committed reaction on the part of the reader.

This book is structured in two sections: in the first part, the theoretical relevance of Trauma Studies in various disciplines is taken into account; in the second part, the focus is on literature and on the ethical importance of style in Martin Amis's *Time's Arrow*.

1. AN INTERDISCIPLINARY THEORETICAL APPROACH TO THE STUDY OF TRAUMA

1.1 A brief history of the studies on trauma

The historical development of the study of trauma is characterized by a waxing and waning of interest[21]. Modern understanding of trauma began in the 1860s with the work of the British physician John Erichsen, who identified the trauma syndrome in victims of railway accidents and ascribed it to a shock of the spinal column[22]. A few years later, German neurologist Hermann Oppenheim named it "traumatic neurosis" and attributed its symptoms to imperceptible organic changes in the brain[23]. For the next fifty years, the emphasis in the study of trauma continued to be on the physiology of shock.

The term trauma acquired a more distinctly psychological meaning in the works of Jean-Martin Charcot, Pierre Janet, Sigmund Freud and others[24]. These turn-of-the-century intellectuals employed the term trauma to refer to the wounding of the mind caused by unexpected emotional shock. Investigations about trauma were focused on the blowing apart of personality caused by extreme fright, and trauma was defined as a memory crisis that troubled the integrity of the self. The traumatized psyche was understood as a system for registering the shocking events outside of ordinary awareness, and the cure for retrieving the forgotten, dissociated or repressed memories was hypnosis, which operated cathartically by bringing them into consciousness and language.

At the beginning of the twentieth century, the interest in trauma declined. However, the outbreak of traumatic neuroses of war during World War I made it unavoidable to recognize the existence of traumatic symptoms, and massive trauma inflicted deliberately on large groups of people by other human beings became a major concern during the First World War. Initially, the symptoms of combat neurosis were considered a physical affliction of the nervous system caused by the concussive effects of exploding shells, but shell shock was also found among soldiers with no physical injuries. Therefore, it had to be admitted that victims of shell shock fell ill not from organic lesions, but from psychical

---

[21] For a more detailed analysis, see R. Leys, *Trauma: A Genealogy*, Chicago: University of Chicago Press, 2000.
[22] J. E. Erichsen, *On Railway and Other Injuries of the Nervous System*, London: Walton & Maberly, 1866.
[23] H. Oppenheim, *Diseases of the Nervous System*, Philadelphia: Lippincott, 1901.
[24] See J. M. Charcot, *Clinical Lectures on Diseases of the Nervous System*, trans. R. Harris, London: Routledge, 1991; P. M. Janet, *Psychological Healing: A Historical and Clinical Study*, New York: Arno Press, 1976; S. Freud, *Beyond the Pleasure Principle*, London: Norton Library, 1961, and *Moses and Monotheism*, New York: Vintage Books, 1955.

causes, and the symptoms of shell shock were re-evaluated as a psychological trauma.

Although the majority of physicians did not recognize the psychic suffering of the shell shocked soldier, a small but increasingly influential minority began to acknowledge the psychogenic nature of war neuroses. Psychoanalysis seemed to be the best approach to the interpretation and treatment of the massive traumas of modern warfare, and psychoanalysts began to develop a theory of trauma which was similar to nineteenth-century theories about female hysteria. Freud, in particular, recognized the importance of the neuroses of World War I for the development of modern theories about trauma:

> A condition has long been known and described which occurs after severe mechanical concussions, railway disasters and other accidents involving a risk to life; it has been given the name of "traumatic neurosis". The terrible war which has just ended gave rise to a great number of illnesses of this kind, but it at least put an end to the temptation to attribute the cause of the disorder to organic lesions of the nervous system brought about by mechanical force.[25]

The interest in trauma declined again between the wars, and massive trauma continued to be seen as an exclusively military affair until the Second World War, when traumatic symptoms started to be observed among civilians. In the aftermath of World War II, the traumas inflicted in concentration camps demanded a new approach to the diagnosis and treatment of psychic trauma. Some independent psychoanalytic studies of the effects of trauma on survivors of the Holocaust identified the existence of a "concentration camp syndrome" or "survivor syndrome". However, there was not a widespread arousal of interest in trauma, because everyone wanted to forget what had happened, and even the survivors did not want to recall the traumatic memories.

A renewed interest in trauma emerged in the 1970s- '80s, after the Vietnam War, thanks to the political struggle by psychiatrists, social workers and other activists to recognize the post-war sufferings of Vietnam War veterans. Finally, the traumatic syndrome was officially acknowledged by the American Psychiatric Association in 1980, in the third edition of the *Diagnostic and Statistical Manual of Mental Disorders*, where the term Post-Traumatic Stress Disorder (PTSD) was adopted for the first time.

The PTSD construct has become a blanket term, and it raises a broad spectrum of issues. On the one hand, PTSD defines the psychic harms associated with certain atrocious experiences of the twentieth century, crucially the Holocaust. On the other hand, the concept of trauma is also applied to much

---

[25] S. Freud, *Beyond the Pleasure Principle*, p. 10.

more questionable experiences, so that the diagnosis of PTSD risks becoming "debased currency"[26]. Therefore, the use of the term trauma raises questions of morality: for example, it has been questioned whether it is appropriate to include in one single concept both individual and collective traumas, and so many various experiences such as genocides, earthquakes, illnesses, railway or car accidents, abortions and sexual abuses.

Freud's description of trauma
Freud is a founding figure in the history of the conceptualization of trauma, because he enhanced the idea of psychic trauma and put the basis for our modern understanding of trauma. The word trauma, from the Greek τραυμα ("*trauma*"), was originally the term for a physical wound, and referred to a rupture of the skin resulting in a catastrophic global reaction of the entire organism. Freud transposed this notion into psychology and the term trauma began to be understood as a wound inflicted not upon the body, but upon the mind. The wound of the mind is not, like the wound of the body, a simple and healable event; it is an event which is experienced too unexpectedly to be fully understood, and is therefore not available to consciousness.

In *Beyond the Pleasure Principle* (1920), Freud posits the existence of a "stimulus barrier" designed to defend the organism against excessive stimuli from the external world. According to Freud, trauma is caused by an extensive breach in the ego's protective shield, and this rupture allows the mind to be flooded with large amounts of stimuli, so that the mind has to face the problem of mastering and binding them:

> We describe as "traumatic" any excitations from outside which are powerful enough to break through the protective shield. [...] an external trauma is bound to provoke a disturbance on a large scale in the functioning of the organism's energy [...]. There is no longer any possibility of preventing the mental apparatus from being flooded with large amounts of stimulus, and another problem arises instead – the problem of mastering the amounts of stimulus which have broken in.[27]

When the ego is caught unprepared to bind additional amounts of energy, its protective shield is breached. The failure of the attempts at mastering and binding the external stimuli, due to the ego's lack of preparedness, produces the symptoms of psychic trauma. Anxiety should protect the psyche's coherence, it is the ego's guard against future shocks, but at the same time it disarrays the ego: anxiety is both cure and cause of trauma.

---

[26] R. Leys, *Trauma*, p. 2.
[27] S. Freud, *Beyond the Pleasure Principle*, pp. 33-34.

Freud also bases his definition of trauma on the concept of latency, a period of time between the accident and the first appearance of the symptoms. In stressing the role of a post-traumatic latency period, Freud made the traumatic experience irreducible to the idea of a purely physiological causal sequence, and argued that it was not the experience itself which acted traumatically, but its delayed revival as a memory.

Since the traumatic event is not fully assimilated at the time it occurs, it returns to haunt the survivor later on. In *Moses and Monotheism* (1939), Freud proposes the concept of latency through the example of the accident:

> It may happen that someone gets away, apparently unharmed, from the spot where he has suffered a shocking accident, for instance a train collision. In the course of the following weeks, however, he develops a series of grave psychical and motor symptoms, which can be ascribed only to his shock [...]. He has developed a "traumatic neurosis". [...] The time that elapsed between the accident and the first appearance of the symptoms is called the "incubation period", a transparent allusion to the pathology of infectious disease. [...] It is the feature which one might term *latency*.[28]

Freud's notion of *Nachträglichkeit*, or "deferred action", brought to conceive trauma as constituted by a dialectic between two events, neither of which was intrinsically traumatic, and a temporal delay or latency that made the past available only by a deferred act of understanding. The first event was not traumatic in itself, because it came too early in childhood to be understood; the second one, which was also not inherently traumatic, triggered a memory of the first event, thereby giving it traumatic meaning. Trauma is thus defined by Freud as the successive movement from an event to its repression to its return. This notion of trauma involves a radical rethinking of the temporality of memory and represents a useful model for reconsidering the relation between memory and trauma and discarding the linear conception of historical time.

Another important characteristic of trauma that Freud first recognized was the surprising literality and non-symbolic nature of traumatic dreams and flashbacks: latency preserves the event in its literality. Therefore, the traumatic dream is the literal return of the event, often against the will of the one it inhabits. The strange connection between the elision of memory and the precision of recall in trauma was first noted by Pierre Janet, and then highlighted by Freud. According to them, traumatic recall remains unchanged to the extent that it has never been fully integrated into understanding.

Trauma is a confrontation with an event that cannot be placed within the schemes of prior knowledge. Therefore, that event continually returns, in its

---

[28] S. Freud, *Moses and Monotheism*, p. 84.

exactness, at a later time. The crucial factor that determines the repetition of trauma is the presence of not-integrated experience, and the compulsion to repeat is related to repression: if a person does not remember, he/she will act out and reproduce the traumatic experience not as a memory but as an action.

Freud also introduces in the notion of psychic trauma the concept of the *unheimlich*, or uncanny, a normative experience that represents something already experienced which has been repressed. The experience of the uncanny represents a form of dialectic between reminiscence and forgetting. The uncanny can also include frightening experiences that cannot be expressed in words (the unthinkable or the unrepresentable). In fact, those who experience massive trauma are faced with an unbelievable and unreal reality, and can no longer believe what they see. They have difficulty in distinguishing between the unreal reality they have survived and the fears that spring from their imagination.

Freud considers the uncanny as a return of what has been repressed. This repression effaces and preserves thoughts: it makes them known through fragmentary manifestations or incomprehensible acts. The uncanny also refers to the sudden appearance of the ambiguous which exists in all that is familiar. An object becomes *unheimlich* when it contains some characteristics of the familiar object, but with a twist that is threatening. When this combination of the familiar and the unfamiliar confronts the ego with a paradox that it cannot solve, the experience becomes traumatic.[29]

Finally, Freud illustrates how a pattern of repetition compulsion governs the lives of those who have undergone traumatic experiences. In *Beyond the Pleasure Principle*, he analyses the peculiar way in which painful events seem to repeat themselves in the lives of certain individuals, who appear as possessed by a fate of catastrophe. Freud turns to literature in order to describe this pattern of suffering.

By narrating the moving story of Tancred and Clorinda told by Torquato Tasso in his epic *Gerusalemme Liberata*, Freud exposes the pattern of repetition compulsion which characterizes traumatic experiences: Tancred unwittingly kills his beloved Clorinda in a duel while she is disguised in the armor of an enemy knight. Later, when he hits with his sword a tall tree in a strange magic forest, blood streams from the cut and the voice of Clorinda, whose soul is imprisoned in the tree, complains that he has wounded her once again. The actions of Tancred represent for Freud "the way that the experience of a trauma repeats itself, exactly and unremittingly, through the unknowing acts of the survivor and against his very will".[30]

As Caruth suggests, the literary significance of Freud's example goes beyond the illustration of repetition compulsion: what is striking in Tancred's story is

---

[29] See S. Freud, *The Uncanny*, London: Penguin, 2003.
[30] S. Freud, *Beyond the Pleasure Principle*, p. 2.

not only the repetition of the wounding, but also the moving voice of Clorinda that cries out, addressing Tancred and thus bearing witness to the past[31]. Therefore, with this literary story Freud suggests that trauma is much more than the simple illness of the wounded psyche: it is the story of a wound that cries out, that addresses us. Since trauma is a crisis that is marked by the ways it simultaneously defies and requires our witness, it cannot be transmitted in a straightforward way, but needs a literary language that at the same time resists and demands our understanding.

Narrative psychology: self and language
Narrative psychology is a branch of psychology, or, better, it is a stance within psychology which emphasizes the interconnections between self and language, sharing with postmodernism the concern with language as a tool for the construction of reality. In particular, narrative psychologists agree with the postmodernist idea that knowledge is determined not by logic or rationality, but by the twists and turns of language.

Since the experience of the self assumes significance only through specific linguistic structures, narrative psychology aims at studying the narratives which constitute selves, and at analyzing the implications of those narratives for individuals and societies. In fact, narrative psychologists consider narrative as the organizing principle for human life: in order to deal with experience, human beings need to construct stories and to listen to the stories of others.

Narrative psychology developed mainly in relation to the psychology of trauma, in the attempt to understand how people adapt and respond to traumatizing events. It underlines the fact that, while traumatic discourse is fragmentary and contradictory, "normal" discourse usually presents a certain degree of coherence, because the human mind has an essentially narrative structure: "human beings think, perceive, imagine, interact and make moral choices according to narrative structures"[32].

Our experience of self, others and the world is embedded within language, and cannot transcend it. There can be different ways of organizing episodes (that is, different kinds of narratives), but what remains fixed is the fact that human beings always seek to impose a narrative structure on the flow of experience, and they need stories as moral guides. As MacIntyre has observed, "deprive children of stories and you will leave them unscripted, anxious stutterers in their actions as in their words"[33]. Therefore, the only way to gain an understanding of human life and society is through stories, fables and parables.

---

[31] C. Caruth, *Unclaimed Experience: Trauma, Narrative and History*, Baltimore: Johns Hopkins University Press, 1996, p. 2.
[32] T. R. Sarbin, *Narrative Psychology*, New York: Praeger, 1986, p. 9.
[33] A. MacIntyre, *After Virtue*, New York: Notre Dame University Press, 1981, p. 54.

The temporal structure that governs human experience is a complex one. As it is commonly known, every story is characterized by two sorts of time: on the one hand, there is the discrete chronological succession of events, and on the other hand, the way in which the story is composed. The mode of time through which we experience events is more similar to the latter one, and it is characterized by "integration, culmination and closure owing to which the story receives a particular configuration"[34]: as Paul Ricoeur has argued, "time becomes human to the extent that it is articulated through a narrative mode"[35]. In fact, we are constantly in search of an emplotment for our life stories: the concept of *narrative identity* intends precisely to indicate that the self comes into being only in the process of telling a life story.

The literary text has often been distinguished from life on the basis that literature displays a higher sense of structure and order: the elements and events making up a literary story have been put there by an author who can eliminate disruptive elements and create coherence thanks to his selective capacity. Life cannot have such a structure because, unlike the author, we do not totally create our materials: we are stuck with what we have in terms of characters, capacities and circumstances. Moreover, we are not describing events which are already completed: we are in the middle of our stories and we cannot be sure of how they will end.

However, individuals can partially determine the course of their own lives: like the author, we can compose the stories of our lives through story plotting and story telling. In fact, we can select or omit certain elements and events both in story plotting, that is, in planning and making decisions, and in story telling, that is, when we narrate ourselves to others. Therefore, since we cannot determine the beginning or the end of our stories, nor choose our materials, our lives do lack the formal order and coherence of literary stories, but at the same time, through story plotting and story telling we can partially determine the course of our lives.

Since Freud, the study of the self has been based on the assumption that mental health corresponds to a coherent narrative account of one's life. Past events are not meaningful in themselves, but are given significance by the configuration of one's narrative, and we do not discover ourselves in narrative; rather, we create ourselves through narrative. In fact, it is only through the process of telling our life stories that we become ethical beings: the self comes to be human only in relation to others.

Trauma causes a radical sense of disorientation, feelings of disintegration and groundlessness, and an existential crisis in which nothing makes sense anymore:

---

[34] M. Crossley, *Introducing Narrative Psychology*, Philadelphia: Open University Press, 2000, p. 49.
[35] P. Ricoeur, *Time and Narrative*, Chicago: Chicago University Press, 1984, p.85.

all this can lead to the breakdown of a coherent life story. What psychotherapy tries to do is precisely to cure trauma by creating a sense of coherence and meaning of one's life: by writing or telling about their traumas, traumatized individuals open themselves up to others. Hence, for traumatized individuals story telling is an act of taking responsibility for the other, an act of bearing witness.

In the contemporary era, the experience of the self is no longer one of unity, wholeness and coherent integrity. By adopting disruptive narrative techniques that subvert the traditional literary conventions, according to which a good novel proceeds in chronological order and has a beginning, a middle and an end, postmodern novels aim precisely at reproducing the fragmentation of the self and the chaotic nature of human experience in the postmodern age.

However, narrative psychology suggests that, on a routine basis, in human life there is more order and coherence than in postmodernist novels. In fact, traumatizing events can be defined as traumas precisely because they do not conform to our normal sense of reality, which has a more ordered structure (or, at least, it is characterized by a struggle to create stability): if traumatized accounts are marked by fragmentation, chaos and disruption of chronology, it is because they deviate from the normal state of narrative, which is usually more coherent. Hence, trauma fiction can indeed be considered as the most apt genre to support the subversive narrative strategies of postmodern literature.

1.2 The social dimension of trauma

Trauma has a social dimension. As Yale sociologist Kai Erikson has argued, there is an analogy between individual and society, and the social fabric can be damaged in the same way as the fabrics of mind and body. The damaged collective organism of a traumatized society can thus be described in the same way as the damaged body or mind of an individual[36]. In fact, although collective trauma "does not have the quality of suddenness normally associated with «trauma»", Erikson claims that "it is a form of shock all the same"[37].

As individual trauma is a blow to the psyche that breaks through the mind's protective shield, collective trauma can be defined as a blow to the basic structures of social life that destroys the bonds between people and damages the sense of communality. However, since populations subjected to collective trauma are affected as groups, rather than as individuals, traumatized communities are somehow different from assemblies of traumatized people: the

---

[36] K. Erikson, "Notes on Trauma and Community", p. 188.
[37] K. Erikson, *Everything in Its Path*, p. 154.

collective trauma suffered by a group is more than the sum of the individual sufferings that make it up.

Culture plays a key role in determining the degree to which traumatized individuals will be affected by trauma. The extent to which trauma will be suffered by an individual who has undergone an extreme experience depends, at least in part, on the society's reactions, and on the cultural and material support offered by social institutions to those who have been traumatized: this puts a specific responsibility on the collectivity. In fact, while in an empathetic society the traumatic symptoms will be alleviated, in a hostile environment there is a risk of re-traumatization. Trauma can thus be socially produced.

Therefore, society should recognize the sufferings of its members and be able to deal with traumatized groups and individuals. As literary historian Sven Kramer notes, "[t]rying to 'close the books' not only ignores the ongoing suffering of trauma victims – it aggravates their suffering as well"[38]. In particular, Kramer argues that the task of coming to terms with collective trauma should be assigned to literature: "just as psychoanalytical treatment liberates an individual from the effects of its psychic wounds, literary 'treatment' through storytelling must liberate a community from its collective trauma"[39]. Literature is thus the means for collectively finding words to express trauma.

Although psychoanalysis is often understood merely as a psychology of the individual, cultural historian Dominick LaCapra underlines how certain psychoanalytical concepts are crucial to understanding the relation between cultures and social groups, and between the present and the past[40]. In fact, the basic psychoanalytic processes of transference, acting-out and working-through undercut the opposition between the individual and society, insofar as they involve "social individuals"[41] with a collective as well as an individual status.

Collective trauma does not just affect the inner world, but also the psychic spaces which relate a person to the outer world, insofar as the process of coming to terms with the past is linked with ethical, social and political concerns: what happens to the individual is not purely personal, but bound up with larger social, political and cultural elements. Therefore, the concepts of psychoanalysis can be applied not only to individuals, but also to social and cultural phenomena. In particular, certain socio-cultural experiences could be seen as a return of the (historically) repressed.

---

[38] S. Kramer, "Talking around Trauma: on the Relationship between Trauma, Narration, and Catharsis in Literature". *TRN-Newsletter 2*, Hamburg Institute for Social Research, June 2004. <http://www.traumaresearch.net/focus2/kramer.htm>.
[39] *Ibid.*
[40] D. LaCapra, *Representing the Holocaust: History, Theory, Trauma*, Ithaca: Cornell University Press, 1996, p. 9.
[41] *Ibid.*

Traumatized individuals perceive trauma as a catastrophic knowledge that cannot be communicated to others. Part of the traumatic experience is precisely the relation to society, which does not want to listen to, or hear about, the testimonies of those who have survived a traumatic experience, because testimony is perceived as an accusation. What Dori Laub has said with reference to the Holocaust could be extended to traumatic experiences in general: the problem of witnessing is that "there [is] no longer an other to which one [can] say 'Thou' in the hope of being heard"[42].

The relation between society and trauma is dynamic and reciprocal: if, on the one hand, the social context influences the self-perception and recovery of the traumatized individuals, on the other hand, the victims as a social group also have an influence on society. In fact, society can be affected by the presence of large traumatized groups: depending on the circumstances, the effects of collective trauma on society can range from the shaping of a stronger collective identity to social disintegration.

Collective trauma has the power to contribute to the shaping of cultural identities: a traumatic event can turn into a *founding trauma*[43] and become the basis for collective identity. The Holocaust, for example, has become a *founding trauma* for contemporary Jewish identity. In this sense, trauma can be considered as a source of communality and it contributes to the creation of social bonds, insofar as it gives the victims a feeling that they are special and unique.

Traumatic experiences often dominate the society's imagery, becoming the main source of communality and contributing to the shaping of collective identities. *Founding traumas* are typical of myths of origin and are present in the mythologized history of every nation: the memory of trauma is a powerful image around which social identities can crystallize. Cultural stories, myths and legends that have as themes the mastery of past traumas represent a resource particularly for those society which are currently undergoing collective trauma.

However, trauma has not only centripetal, but also centrifugal tendencies: traumatizing experiences can lead to social disintegration too. In a "normal" context, culture should generate a system of support that lessens the impact of trauma and protects individuals from the disruptive impact of trauma, in order to avoid the disintegration of the social structures that hold society together. Yet, collective traumas have the power to disrupt the continuity and integrity of the cultural system: these disruptive forces may be so unexpected as to damage the structures that hold society together and overwhelm society's restorative capacity, leaving its members vulnerable to traumatic symptoms.

---

[42] D. Laub, "Truth and Testimony: the Process and the Struggle", in C. Caruth (ed.), *Trauma: Explorations in Memory*, p. 66.
[43] D. LaCapra, "Trauma, Absence, Loss", *Critical Inquiry* 25.4 (1999), p. 712.

Human beings are normally surrounded by layers of trust, and social structures work to camouflage the dangers of the world. However, in a traumatized society culture no longer screens out signs of peril, so that the world appears as a place full of dangers. Traumatized people feel very vulnerable because society has failed to protect them against trauma, or even contributed to the traumatic event. Collective trauma can thus bring the individual to realize that society is no longer an effective source of support and protection for him/her. This, in turn, can lead to a loss of confidence in family and society, and to a disintegration of the individual's trust in social structures and institutions.

Chosen trauma and transgenerational transmission of trauma
Psychiatrist Vamik Volkan has made an important contribution to our understanding of the relation between trauma and society by developing the term *chosen trauma* to describe what happens when society is unable to mourn past losses. According to Volkan, when mourning fails, social groups may develop a collective representation of themselves as victims, and transform losses into cultural narratives which become an integral part of the social identity:

> I use the term *chosen trauma* to describe the collective memory of a calamity that once befell on a group's ancestors. It is, of course, more than a simple recollection: it is a shared mental representation of the event, which includes realistic information, fantasized expectations, intense feelings, and defenses against unacceptable thoughts.
>
> Since a group does not choose to be victimized, some of my colleagues have taken exception to the term *chosen trauma*. But I maintain that the word *chosen* fittingly reflects a large group's unconsciously defining identity by the transgenerational transmission of injured selves infused with the memory of the ancestors' trauma.[44]

When a collective identity is marked by a *chosen trauma*, the recognition that one belongs to some group is accompanied by sense of humiliation and self-blame, and membership in that community is associated with failure, moral inadequacy, shame and guilt. For example, Jews were destroyed by Nazis precisely because they were Jewish: it was their Jewishness that led to the trauma of the Holocaust. Of course, Jews did not choose to be victimized, but they mythologized what had occurred, and unconsciously chose to define their identity by referring to the trauma of the Holocaust. The Jewish identity is thus shaped by a *chosen trauma*.

Chosen trauma generates feelings of pride and revenge, and these feelings can be transmitted through culturally mediated forms, such as cultural narratives and

---
[44] V. Volkan, "Chosen Trauma: Unresolved Mourning", in V. Volkan, *Bloodlines: From Ethnic Pride to Ethnic Terrorism*, Boudler, Colorado: Westview Press, 1998, p. 48.

myths of origins, from one generation to the next, because there is an unconscious expectation that the next generation will complete both the task of mourning and the reversal of humiliation. Trauma can thus be passed on to others and its effects can last longer than one generation. In fact, although the basic model for the transmission of trauma is a face-to-face encounter between a traumatized victim and an empathetic listener, trauma can also be transmitted trans-generationally across space and time, that is, from one generation to the next, so that the memory of trauma may haunt ensuing generations who have never experienced it directly.

Trauma theorist Cathy Caruth has extended the concept of transgenerational transmission of trauma by claiming that "trauma is never simply one's own"[45]: everyone can be imagined as receiving a trauma that he or she never experienced directly. According to her, it is the written text that transmits traumas across generations: through texts, later generations can gain access to the memory of ancestors' trauma and turn it into a *chosen trauma* that can shape their collective identity. Caruth argues that the experience of trauma can be shared by victims and non-victims alike, and that the sufferings of the survivor can be appropriated by others. Therefore, she generalizes the notion of trauma to include not only victims, but also bystanders, secondary witnesses, and maybe even perpetrators: for Caruth history is "the history of a trauma"[46], and the effects of trauma can be spread throughout an entire society or community.

The intergenerational transmission of trauma is a manifestation of the collective impact of trauma on society, and it reinforces the idea, inherent in the concept of *chosen trauma*, that trauma can shape cultural identities: if the trauma experienced by one generation can be transmitted to later generations, the traumatic memories inherited from ancestors may become the basis for a collective identity.

Primary and secondary traumatization
The tendency of traumatized individuals to repeat the past can have contagious effects. Some trauma theorists understand history as inherently traumatic and insist on the fact that the effects of trauma can affect everyone. In particular, psychiatrist Dori Laub argues that an empathetic listener may experience a modified version of the survivor's trauma:

> The listener to trauma comes to be a participant and a co-owner of the traumatic event: through his very listening, he comes to partially experience the trauma in himself. [...] The listener has to feel the victim's victories, defeats and silences, know them from within [...]. The listener, however, is also a separate human being and will

---
[45] C. Caruth, *Unclaimed Experience*, p. 24.
[46] *Ibid.*, p. 15.

experience hazards and struggles of his own, while carrying out his function of a witness to the trauma witness. While overlapping, to a degree, with the experience of the victim, he nonetheless does not become the victim [...].[47]

> Bearing witness to a trauma is, in fact, a process which includes the listener. For the testimonial process to take place, there needs to be a bonding, the intimate and total presence of an *other-* in the position of one who hears.[48]

Laub thus maintains that interviewers and analysts of traumatized people may undergo *secondary traumatization*.

Other trauma theorists have responded warily to Laub's understanding of the role of the listener: for example, Kalì Tal has objected to Laub's interpretation of trauma because it "makes no distinction between the primary trauma suffered by the Holocaust survivor and the sort of secondary stress suffered by the testimonial audience"[49]. However, Laub does not seem to be conflating primary and secondary traumatization, but simply arguing that there is an empathetic relation between witness and listener.

Geoffrey Hartman has also criticized Laub's "positive view"[50] of secondary trauma. Nonetheless, he admits the possibility of a traumatization of secondary witnesses, and points to the risks of an over-exposure to traumatic accounts:

> The media have turned all of us into involuntary bystanders of atrocities, reported graphically and hourly. From this media-reportage of traumatic events, from this fluent and relentless transmission of violent images, a "secondary trauma" could arise, this time affecting the spectators of our own Roman Circuses. Though in the ordinary course of life everyone is exposed to sights of death and suffering, what is so worrisome is the routine exposure, one that habituates and fascinates and tends to produce feelings of indifference.[51]

According to Hartman, testimony as a social act avoids the danger of secondary trauma, insofar as the narrative that emerges through the encounter between witness and interviewer does not present "a series of fixed images that assault the eye [n]or an impersonal historical digest"[52].

---

[47] S. Felman and D. Laub, *Testimony: Crises of Witnessing in Literature, Psychoanalysis and History*, New York: Routledge, 1992, pp. 57-8.
[48] *Ibid.*, p. 70.
[49] K. Tal, *Worlds of Hurt: Reading the Literatures of Trauma*, Cambridge, New York: Cambridge University Press, 1996, p. 56.
[50] G. Hartman, *The Longest Shadow: In the Aftermath of the Holocaust*, New York: Palgrave MacMillan, 2002, p. 165, footnote 10.
[51] *Ibid.*, p. 152.
[52] *Ibid.*, p. 154.

Historian Dominick LaCapra insists on the difference between primary and secondary traumatization, that is, between experienced and transmitted trauma. Even though the existence of some form of secondary traumatization is commonly acknowledged by trauma theorists, the situation of those who have personally experienced a traumatic event should indeed be distinguished from that of other people not directly involved. LaCapra is against an "overextension of the concept of trauma"[53] and underlines the dangers of over-identification:

> If we who have not been severely traumatized by experiences involving massive losses go to the extreme of identifying [...] with the victim and survivor, our horizon may unjustifiably become that of the survivor, if not the victim at least as we imagine her or him to be. In other words we may come to feel that it is enough if we simply survive and, at most, bear witness. [...] We may even undergo surrogate victimage – something that may at times be unavoidable but, in terms of ethical, social, and civic responsibility, is open to question, particularly in its effects in the public sphere.[54]

LaCapra is thus warning us against "the indiscriminate generalization of the category of survivor and the overall conflation of history or culture with trauma"[55]. In particular, he questions the desire of secondary witnesses to identify with the victim and underlines how the otherness of the other must always be respected: there is clearly a major difference between the experience of Holocaust survivors and that of video-testimonies' viewers.

Moreover, LaCapra wants to make clear that the historian is at most "a secondary witness through empathy"[56], that is, he/she may not assume the voice of the victim. In fact, secondary witnesses should respond ethically to survivors' testimonies: some form of empathetic unsettlement is indeed required, but empathy should not become identification, nor give way to "vicarious victimhood"[57]. LaCapra highlights the difference between primary and secondary traumatization by referring to the distinctions between empathy and identification, absence and loss, structural and historical trauma, acting-out and working-through.

Empathy is often mistakenly conflated with identification, but it should rather be understood as "an affective relation, rapport, or bond with the other recognized and respected as other"[58]. The difference between empathy and identification lies in the fact that, while the first involves an affective response

---

[53] D. LaCapra, *Writing*, p. 102.
[54] *Ibid.*, p. 211.
[55] *Ibid.*, p. xi.
[56] *Ibid.*, p. 97, footnote 10.
[57] D. LaCapra, "Trauma, Absence, Loss", p. 697.
[58] D. LaCapra, *Writing*, pp. 212-13.

linked with critical judgment, the latter has no sense of emotional distance. According to LaCapra, empathy is desirable in front of traumatic events only when it does not go to the extreme of full identification. Identifying with the victim "to the point of making oneself a surrogate victim who has a right to the victim's voice"[59], without recognizing that the trauma of the other is not identical to a first-person experience of traumatization, is indeed a dubious way of approaching traumatized accounts. Therefore, an attentive secondary witness should open him- or herself to empathetic unsettlement, but avoid identification: this means putting oneself in the other's position, while recognizing at the same time the otherness of the victim, thus not taking his or her place.

Empathy can be an important component of research insofar as it can enhance empirical investigation and help us understand traumatic events and victims. The question of empathy poses the problem of how to write (about) traumatic events without confusing one's own voice with the victim's. In fact, empathy has stylistic effects, and it can influence the modes of historical, testimonial and fictional representation in different ways. Generalizing, it is possible to say that empathy raises doubts about positivistic accounts and *grand narratives* that seek full closure, thus inhibiting harmonizing and totalizing (hi)stories.

In order to distinguish those who have experienced trauma directly from secondary witnesses, LaCapra also refers to the distinctions between absence and loss, and between structural trauma and historical trauma. He considers absence as situated on a trans-historical level: therefore, "absence is not an event and does not imply tenses (past, present, or future)"[60]. On the contrary, loss is situated on a historical level and it is specific. Since loss is the consequence of a particular event and does not affect everyone, it cannot be conflated with absence, which appears in all societies and is something constitutive of every human existence:

> Absence (not loss) applies to ultimate foundations in general, notably to metaphysical grounds (including the human being as origin of meaning and value). In this sense, absence is the absence of an absolute that should not itself be absolutized and fetishized such that it becomes an object of fixation and absorbs, mystifies, or downgrades the significance of particular historical losses.[61]

Absence cannot be the cause of a primary traumatization: in fact, "in terms of absence, one may recognize that one cannot lose what one never had"[62]. By

---

[59] D. LaCapra, "Trauma, Absence, Loss", p. 710.
[60] *Ibid.*, p. 698.
[61] *Ibid.*, p. 699.
[62] *Ibid.*, p. 699.

contrast, loss indicates something that should be there but is missing, and it may or may not be traumatic, depending on the nature of the event that caused it.

LaCapra observes how the concepts of absence and loss have often been conflated, and highlights the fact that his distinction has an ethical and political value. When the distinction between absence and loss is blurred, the force of a particular historical loss (for example, that of the Holocaust) may be obfuscated, and its significance over-generalized. According to LaCapra, the ideas that "all history is trauma, or that we all share a pathological public sphere or a 'wound culture'"[63] could lead to believe that everyone, including perpetrators, is a victim.

However, I do not think that Cathy Caruth's claim that trauma is "a symptom of history"[64] goes beyond the limits of ethics, because it does not attempt to justify or absolve perpetrators, but simply extends the notion of trauma to society as a whole. Although there is indeed a difference between absence and loss, between primary and secondary trauma, it should still be acknowledged that, as I have already pointed out, collective trauma can be transmitted across space and time, and spread throughout an entire society, hence affecting also those who have not experienced it directly.

A related issue is LaCapra's distinction between structural and historical trauma. While structural trauma appears in different ways in all societies and all lives, historical trauma is specific and not everyone is subject to it. Although the period of latency makes the traumatic experience elusive in both cases, in historical trauma it is nonetheless possible to locate the traumatizing event: historical trauma has a specificity that impedes its incorporation within structural trauma, which is not an event, but simply "an anxiety-producing condition of possibility related to the potential for historical traumatization"[65] that is inherent in every human existence. Therefore, although structural trauma may be considered as a precondition for historical trauma, the tendency to generalize structural trauma so that it assumes the significance of historical trauma risks reducing the specificity and thus the relevance of the latter.

Finally, LaCapra adopts the psychoanalytical distinction between acting-out and working-through in order to further underline the difference between primary and secondary traumatization. Acting-out is linked to repetition: traumatized people tend to relive the past, to be haunted by ghosts, and thus to repeat the trauma in the present as if they were still in the past. The process of working-through is itself related to repetition too, but it works against the repetition compulsion of acting-out. In fact, while in acting-out the victim performatively relives the past as if it was present, and the past hauntingly

---

[63] Ibid., p. 705.
[64] C. Caruth, "Trauma and Experience", p. 5.
[65] D. LaCapra, "Trauma, Absence, Loss", p. 712.

returns as the repressed, working-through allows some critical distance, so that the past is made available for conscious recall.

The recent tendency to valorize trauma has led to prefer acting-out, considered as a way of preventing harmonization, over working-through, which is understood as aiming to closure and full cure. Traumatized people may resist working-through because of a "fidelity to trauma, a feeling that one must somehow keep faith with it"[66]: the bond with the dead invests trauma with value, and creates a desire to remain within trauma. However, working-through does not mean forgetting the past, but coming to terms with trauma, "distancing oneself from haunting revenants, renewing an interest in life, and being able to engage memory in more critically tested senses"[67], without betraying those who were overwhelmed by the traumatic event.

This kind of socially engaged memory allows the victims to distinguish between past and present: when trauma has been worked through, the past is available for conscious recall, and it can be narrated in a variety of ways. This allows some objectivity, critical judgment, and ethical responsibility, including consideration for others: that is, by working-through one becomes an ethical and political agent.

On the contrary, when the victim is possessed by the past and acts out a repetition compulsion, he or she is incapable of ethically responsible behaviour. Traumatized people who have not worked through their trauma are not able to consciously recall their memories, and the acting-out of the trauma is performed in exactly the same way every time, regardless of the audience or of the context. Nonetheless, acting-out may be a necessary condition of working-through: the acting-out of trauma in victims and empathy in secondary witnesses do not necessarily inhibit working-through.

Acting-out and working-through can thus be seen as related parts of a process. In fact, there is not a binary opposition between working-through as full cure and redemption, and acting-out as staying within trauma and symptomatic repetition compulsion: working-through could represent a means for *writing about trauma*, that is, reconstructing the past as objectively as possible, which is the aim of historiography, while acting-out could be the means for *writing trauma*[68], that is, performatively enacting or reliving trauma in artistic practice, which is precisely a characteristic of literature.

---

[66] D. LaCapra, *Writing*, p. 20.
[67] *Ibid.*, p. 90.
[68] *Ibid.*, p. 186.

1.3 Trauma and memory

Memory is a constructive process. Remembering depends on previous knowledge and on existing mental schemes, which determine to what extent new information is integrated: new experiences can only be interpreted in the light of prior frameworks of understanding. However, intense emotions interfere with proper information processing: while familiar and expectable events are automatically assimilated, traumatic experiences cannot be fitted into existing meaning schemas and must be stored in a memory system different from that of ordinary memory. The lack of integration and the impairment of appropriate categorization of experience are thus typical features of trauma.

Pierre Janet (1859-1947) was a pioneer in the study of trauma and memory. He analyzed how the human mind processes memories and distinguished between two kinds of memory: narrative memory and traumatic memory. According to Janet,

> memory [...] is the action of telling a story [...]. The teller must not only know how to [narrate it], but must also know how to associate that happening with the other events of his life [...]. Strictly speaking, one who retains a fixed idea of a happening cannot be said to have a "memory" of the happening. It is only for convenience that we speak of it as a "traumatic memory".[69]

Narrative memory involves the ability to be aware of the events and verbally narrate them; it is flexible, semantic and symbolic. The accounts of narrative memories have an intended audience, can be performed in a variety of ways and adapted to the circumstances, that is, they can be expanded or contracted according to social demands. Therefore, narrative memory is a social act.

On the contrary, traumatic memory is not adaptive, but inflexible, timeless and invariable: it consists of fixed images and sensations that are not placed in time, and thus not transformed into a coherent story. Traumatic memory is possessed by the past, and it is not altered by the passage of time, because trauma fixes the moment in memory: when the past is relived in traumatic memory, there is no difference between then and now. The acting-out of traumatic memory is not addressed to anyone: it has no social component, because it is not revised in order to fit social expectations.

Moreover, while narrative memory is subject to voluntary control, traumatic memory is rigidly tied to the specific traumatic situation: it is evoked automatically in particular contexts, but it cannot be retrieved at will in normal conditions. Trauma is thus mainly a disorder of remembering and of forgetting: the paradox inherent in traumatic memory is that the traumatized person suffers

---

[69] P. Janet, *Psychological Healing*, pp. 661-3.

from amnesia, but at the same time he or she seems to remember the traumatic event with too much vividness and accuracy. Traumatic re-enactments do not constitute a narration because they lack awareness of the past as past and a conscious re-elaboration of the events. Fragments of the unintegrated traumatic experience often manifest themselves in the form of compulsive and unconscious repetitions of the past: "the very nature of a traumatic memory is to be dissociated, and to be stored initially as sensory fragments that have no linguistic components"[70].

Trauma is wordless and cannot be expressed in linguistic terms: it creates "a structural deficit, wound, or 'hole' in the mind where representation ought to be"[71]. However, it is not entirely mute: traumatic memories are organized on different levels of information processing, such as visual images or somatic sensations, that lie outside symbolic-semantic representation. Hence, although trauma does indeed involve a loss of capacity for narrativization and self-representation, it does not cause the loss of all speech.

A traumatic experience can be integrated into consciousness only if the victim is able to consciously recollect it and narrate it. This implies a transformation of traumatic memory into narrative memory, a memory that can produce a flexible and self-conscious narrative. According to Cathy Caruth, such a process inevitably falsifies the traumatic origin: "the capacity to remember is also the capacity to elide or distort"[72]. In fact, once traumatic memory is transformed into narrative memory, the traumatic event is no longer accessible as an individual entity, and the memory of it will be distorted: "The transformation of the trauma into a narrative memory that allows the story to be verbalized and communicated [...] may lose both the precision and the force that characterizes traumatic recall"[73]. Caruth thus understands trauma as standing outside all knowledge and beyond all representation: according to her, traumatic memory can never be brought into recollection and self-representation, because trauma "is itself constituted by its lack of integration into consciousness"[74], and thus defies all possibilities for representation.

Neurobiologist Bessel Van der Kolk agrees with Caruth in arguing that the order and coherence of narrative memory threaten the essential incomprehensibility of trauma, which risks losing its force and impact: "once flexibility is introduced, the traumatic memory starts losing its power over

---

[70] B. Van der Kolk, "Trauma and Memory", in B. Van der Kolk (ed.), *Traumatic Stress: The Effects of Overwhelming Experience on Mind, Body, and Society*, New York: The Guilford Press, 1996, p. 289.
[71] R. Leys, *Trauma*, p. 249.
[72] C. Caruth, "Recapturing the Past: Introduction", in C. Caruth (ed.), *Trauma: Explorations in Memory*, pp. 153-4.
[73] *Ibid.*, p. 153.
[74] *Ibid.*, p. 152.

current experience"[75]. Therefore, Caruth and Van der Kolk suggest for trauma a form of memory that does not capitulate to closure and coherence, but preserves traumatic disruption and discontinuity, and ask "whether it is not a sacrilege of traumatic experience to play with the reality of the past"[76].

Collective memory

Memory is usually considered as an individual phenomenon. However, society plays a fundamental role in shaping and transmitting memory: remembering is not only an individual process, but it is also culturally and socially mediated. In order to be interpretable and communicable, the individual memory-images need to be verbalized and emplotted, that is, translated into language and transformed into a narrative: this transformation can only occur through social interaction.

Individual memories are constituted within a collectively shared symbolic order and intersubjectively linked to the memories of society as a whole. Personal remembrance is influenced by collective processes and informed by socially organized representations of the past: society determines what is memorable, and how it has to be remembered. Therefore, memory is a collective phenomenon.

In the 1940s-50s, Maurice Halbwachs developed a theory of collective memory that shifted the focus from the biological structure of memory to the cultural and social frameworks that influence memory's recollection and transmission:

> It is in society that people normally acquire memories. It is also in society that they recall, recognize, and localize their memories. [...] Most of the time, when I remember, it is others who spur me on; their memory comes to the aid of mine and mine relies on theirs. [...] There is no point in seeking where they are preserved in my brain or in some nook in my mind to which I alone have access: for they are recalled to me externally, and the groups to which I am a part give me the means to reconstruct them [...]. It is in this sense that there exists a collective memory and social frameworks for memory; it is to the degree that our individual thought places itself in these frameworks and participates in this memory that it is capable of the act of recollection.[77]

According to Halbwachs, memory has no substance outside its social context: individual memories are accessible only through their social actualizations and

---

[75] B. Van Der Kolk, "The Intrusive Past: the Flexibility of Memory and the Engraving of Trauma", in C. Caruth (ed.), *Trauma: Explorations in Memory*, p. 178.
[76] *Ibid.*, p. 179.
[77] M. Halbwachs, *On Collective Memory*, Chicago: University of Chicago Press, 1992, p. 38.

collective representations. Therefore, memory is never really individual, because it is always recollected within the framework of a certain social group. Cultural formations, such as texts, rituals and monuments, preserve the memory of fateful events of the past: in order to be transmitted within the cultural heritage of a society, collectively shared knowledge needs crystallizing in institutionalized cultural formations. Collective memory allows social groups to perpetuate their culture by maintaining the myths and traditions that represent the "spirit" of a society and from which a group derives its unity and peculiarity. In particular, literary texts contribute to the construction of a society's collective memory by facilitating the fixation of an event in collective memory.

As Halbwachs has illustrated, in society individuals can retrieve their recollections and transform their memory-images into concepts. However, society also exercises a power of manipulation over individuals: it intervenes in the individuals' memory and molds it according to its needs. In fact, collective memory represents the past in the light of the needs of the present and selects, reconstructs and organizes the events according to the will of some social group – usually the dominant one – endowing them with political meaning.

Therefore, collective memory is imbricated in political structures and produces narratives that support group interests: "[m]emory and its representations touch [...] upon questions of identity, of nationalism, of power and authority"[78]. History thus becomes "a tool for the ideological and moralistic needs of society, [...] a fabricated narrative [...] in the service of social-ideological needs"[79].

Geoffrey Hartman proposed the notion of "public memory" to define a modern, politicized version of collective memory: since official history is always written by the victors, "who consider public memory part of the spoils and do not hesitate to rewrite history"[80], public memory is a "falsified memory" promoting "an official story that seeks to reawaken ancient hatreds"[81]. According to Hartman, "cultural memory is an abstraction that has to be reconceptualized all the time. [...] it includes a continuous reflection on itself. [...] The public memory, by contrast, is media-driven and myopic"[82]. Moreover, while traditional collective memory was conceived as "a 'living deposit' preserved outside academic or written history"[83], public memory is imposed from above by dominant institutions and expressed in cold and detached narratives and artefacts.

---

[78] E. Said, "Invention, Memory, and Place", *Critical Inquiry* 26.2 (2000), p. 176.
[79] N. Gedi, and E. Yigal, "Collective Memory – What is it?", *History and Memory* 8.1 (1996), p. 41-2.
[80] G. Hartman, *The Longest Shadow*, p. 101.
[81] *Ibid.*, p. 111.
[82] G. Hartman, *Scars of the Spirit*, pp. 200-2.
[83] G. Hartman, *The Longest Shadow*, p. 106.

Memory narratives that shape collective identities are usually normalizing, nationalistic and patriotic. They aim at creating a generalized consensus by representing the past in idealized terms, as a uniform and heroic past. Pierre Nora refers to such expressions of official public memory as "dominant sites":

> Dominant sites are spectacles, celebrations of triumph. They are imposing as well as generally imposed from above by the government or some official organization, and are typically cold and solemn, like official ceremonies. One doesn't visit such places, one is summoned to them.[84]

Commemorative narratives and dominant sites tend to focus on special events, charged with symbolic meaning and represented as turning points in the history of the group. Official history, promoted by institutions of power, manipulates memory and erases the subversive or heterogeneous facts:

> A war is always going on to modify memory. [...] such warfare leads to an institutionalized and bogus recollection, a churlish denial of the history of others [...], or an artificially inseminated perspective. A single authorized narrative then simplifies not just history but the only *active* communal memory we have, made of such traditional materials as legends, poetry, dances, songs, festivals, and recitations, the sum of which helps to define a "culture".[85]

According to Hartman, art as a performative medium has a chance to transmit the inheritance of this "*active* communal memory", because it can provide a counterforce to the falsified and monolithic official history:

> [Literature] counteracts the impersonality and instability of public memory, on the one hand, and, on the other the determinism and fundamentalism of a collective memory based on identity politics. Literature creates an institution of its own, more personal and focused than public memory yet less monologic than the memorializing fables common to ethnic or nationalist affirmation.[86]

---

[84] P. Nora, "Between Memory and History: *Les Lieux de Mémoire*", *Representations* 26 (1989), p. 18.
[85] G. Hartman, *The Longest Shadow*, p. 104.
[86] *Ibid.*, p. 107.

1.4 Trauma and testimony

Geoffrey Hartman describes "the genre, or rather the collective archive, of survivor testimonies"[87] as

> an extracanonical representation [...] suspended between history and memory, suspended also between literature and documentary, whose subject is consistently the daily response to terror, and which provides the lineaments of that sublime yet ordinary story that is a necessity and not an indulgence if we still believe in educating the imagination.[88]

Testimony is the crucial mode for representing the traumas of history: its role in post-Holocaust literature is a central one. "We live in an era of testimony"[89], says Hartman. Of course, testimony was not *invented* in the post-Holocaust era, but the testimonies of Holocaust survivors represented the emergence of a new mode of writing all the same: in the words of Elie Wiesel, "[i]f the Greeks invented tragedy, the Romans the epistle, and the Renaissance the sonnet, our generation invented a new literature, that of testimony"[90].

Most Holocaust survivors have a commitment to bear witness, because they feel that their testimony cannot be substituted or represented by someone else's: if the testimony is reported by another, it loses its function as such. Thus, the witness's speech is irreplaceable:

> Testimony [...] is not simply (as we commonly perceive it) the observing, the recording, the remembering of an event, but an utterly unique and irreplaceable topographical *position* with respect to an occurrence. [...] it is the uniqueness of the *performance of a story* which is constituted by the fact that, like an oath, it cannot be carried out by anybody else [...] The uniqueness of the narrative performance of the testimony in effect proceeds from the witness's irreplaceable performance of the act of seeing – from the uniqueness of the witness's "seeing with his/her own eyes." [...] In the legal, philosophical, and epistemological tradition of the Western world, witnessing is based on, and is formally defined by, first-hand seeing.[91]

---

[87] *Ibid.*, p. 122.
[88] *Ibid.*
[89] *Ibid.*
[90] E. Wiesel, "The Holocaust as Literary Inspiration", in E. Wiesel, et al., *Dimensions of the Holocaust*, Evanston: Northwestern University Press, 1977, p. 9.
[91] S. Felman, "In an Era of Testimony: Claude Lanzmann's *Shoah*", *Yale French Studies* 97 (2000), pp. 105-6.

Paul Celan poetically expresses what Shoshana Felman calls the "radically unique, noninterchangeable, and solitary burden"[92] of the witness, by claiming: "Niemand/ zeugt für/ den Zeugen" ("Noone/ bears witness for the/ witness")[93]. Similarly, in "The Loneliness of God" Elie Wiesel declares:

> If someone else could have written my stories, I would not have written them. I have written them in order to testify. My role is the role of the witness [...] Not to tell, or to tell another story, is [...] to commit perjury"[94].

And Primo Levi in *Survival in Auschwitz* states:

> The need to tell our story to "the rest", to make "the rest" participate in it, had taken on for us, before our liberation and after, the character of an immediate and violent impulse, to the point of competing with our other elementary needs.[95]

Moreover, if we consider that the Nazis devoted extensive effort to concealing and erasing all traces of the crimes they were perpetrating, the responsibility to remember, record and transmit those crimes becomes even stronger.

Testimony is a form of responsible speech that *addresses* the other, and it offers the reader or listener the possibility of a personal connection with events in which he or she was not directly involved. The survivor has a responsibility to bear witness both for those who died and for those who were not there at the time of the traumatic event: "the *appointment* to bear witness is [...] an appointment [...] to speak *for* others and *to* others"[96].

Therefore, testimony has not only a personal moral value, but also a social relevance:

> To bear witness is to take responsibility for truth [...]. To testify – before a court of Law or before the court of history and of the future; to testify, likewise, before an audience of readers or spectators – is more than simply to report a fact or an event or to relate what has been lived, recorded and remembered. Memory is conjured here essentially in order to *address* another, to impress upon a listener, to *appeal* to a

---

[92] S. Felman, "Education and Crisis, or the Vicissitudes of Teaching", in C. Caruth (ed.), *Trauma: Explorations in Memory*, p. 15.
[93] P. Celan, "Ashes-Glory", in P. Celan, *Selections*, trans. P. Joris, Berkeley: University of California Press, 2005. [Trans. "Aschenglorie"].
[94] E. Wiesel, "Bdiduto shel elohim", *Dvar Hashavu'a*, Tel Aviv: 1984. Qtd. and trans. in S. Felman, "In an Era of Testimony", p. 103.
[95] P. Levi, *Survival in Auschwitz: the Nazi Assault on Humanity*, trans. S. Woolf, New York: Touchstone, 1996, p. 9. [Trans. from *Se questo è un uomo*, Torino: Einaudi, 1958].
[96] S. Felman, "Education and Crisis", p. 15.

community. [...] To testify is thus not merely to narrate but to commit oneself, and to commit the narrative, to others: to *take responsibility* – in speech – for history or for the truth of an occurrence, for something which, by definition, goes beyond the personal in having general (nonpersonal) validity and consequences.[97]

In our culture, testimony has been invested with truth-making powers: the function of testimonial literature is often believed to be that of establishing the facts of the Holocaust, of proving that it happened, and "true testimony" is often conceived as a transparent layer through which the original event can be disclosed. However, the post-structuralist claim that the meaning of a text is never transparent has challenged this interpretation. Accordingly, trauma theorists argue that the meaning of testimony should be relocated in the survivor's subjectivity.

The truth of a traumatic event only exists in the individual's psyche, in his or her inner experience of trauma: testimony bears witness precisely to this trauma. Therefore, the value of testimony does not lie in its power to document the facts, but in the survivor's traumatic memory of the facts: by bearing witness, survivors do not turn into historians, but simply become "human witnesses to a dehumanizing situation"[98]. Testimony requires an attentive, empathetic and compassionate audience:

> For the testimonial process to take place, there needs to be a bonding, the intimate and total presence of an *other* – in the position of the one who hears. Testimonies are not monologues; they cannot take place in solitude. The witnesses are talking to *somebody*: to somebody they have been waiting for for a long time.[99]

It is the encounter between survivor and listener that makes the very act of witnessing possible: "this joint responsibility is the source of the reemerging truth"[100]. Testimony is thus a dialogue between the survivor and an audience, a "lived performance for witness and listener alike"[101]: the witness addresses us, and we have a duty to pay attention.

At this point, it should already be clear that witnessing is a collective, social act. The meaning of testimony is located more on a public than on a private level: rather than expressing the author's individuality, testimony is a vehicle of

---

[97] S. Felman, "In an Era of Testimony", pp. 103-4.
[98] G. Hartman, *The Longest Shadow*, p. 136.
[99] S. Felman, and D. Laub, *Testimony*, pp. 70-1.
[100] D. Laub, "Truth and Testimony", p. 69.
[101] F. I. Zeitlin, "The Vicarious Witness: Belated Memory and Authorial Presence in Recent Holocaust Literature", *History and Memory* 10.2 (1998), p. 9.

collective memory, a dialogue between past, present and future, and a process of reconciliation of both listener and survivor with the past.

The overwhelming impact of trauma puts to test the limits of testimony, thus questioning the very limits of reality and the possibility of truth. Traumatic memory, characterized by a lack of integration into the memory system, exerts such a pressure on testimonial narratives as to destroy chronology and hinder coherence and closure. Therefore, the disruptions, gaps and silences of traumatic (testimonial) narratives represent a possibility for communicating the crisis of truth of the postmodern era.

Crises of witnessing

The post-Holocaust era is characterized by a failure of representation: the Holocaust is considered to be unspeakable because it radically exceeds our capacity to grasp it. Trauma destroys the ordinary frameworks of understanding and mechanisms of memory, returning belatedly as a compulsion repetition. Therefore, it cannot be represented in traditional, coherent narrative forms: the victim cannot symbolize trauma, but only perform, re-enact or re-experience it in a disrupted form[102].

Thus, trauma carries within it a *crisis of witnessing*[103]: in our post-traumatic era, witnessing itself has undergone a major trauma. "Testimony and trauma struggle with, against, each other"[104], says Hartman. Traumatic experiences are inaccessible; they resist analysis and defy any attempt to fully comprehend them. At the heart of trauma, there is an impossibility to know and tell. Therefore, "trauma opens up and challenges us to a new kind of listening, the witnessing, precisely, *of impossibility*"[105].

The Holocaust has been defined as an event without a witness, because it literally erased its witnesses, creating a historical gap in testimony[106]. During the Holocaust, no witnesses could be brought into being: while potential outside witnesses refused to see, and thus failed to occupy their position as witnesses, those who were inside the event were not able to make sense of the events and so to produce a coherent and meaningful testimony. In fact, as Geoffrey Hartman underlines by referring to Primo Levi's observations in *The Drowned and the Saved*, in the camps "almost none of the inmates had an extensive view of what was happening"[107].

One of the aims of the Nazis was that of making sure that the survivors would be unable to testify, or that, should they speak, no one would believe them. The

---

[102] C. Caruth, "Trauma and Experience", pp. 3-11.
[103] See S. Felman, and D. Laub, *Testimony*, 1992.
[104] G. Hartman, *Scars of the Spirit*, p. 88.
[105] C. Caruth, "Trauma and Experience", p. 10.
[106] D. Laub, "Truth and Testimony", pp. 65-9.
[107] G. Hartman, *Scars of the Spirit*, p. 86.

atrocious sufferings annihilated the victims, and thus undid the very possibility of witnessing: "it was [...] the very circumstance of *being inside the event* that made unthinkable the very notion that a witness could exist"[108]. The inconceivability of the facts of the Holocaust caused not only a disbelief in the victims' accounts on the part of listeners, but also a distrust of their own memories on the part of survivors themselves: "the inherently incomprehensible *and* deceptive psychological structure"[109] of the Holocaust, and the unwillingness of the outside world to receive the testimony, compromised the very possibility of witnessing.

The crisis of witnessing brought about by the traumatic experience of the Holocaust has also been precipitated by the recognition that those who survived and so could testify were "inadequate witnesses because of their restricted angle of view, but also because the few who managed to see more had inhabited a 'grey zone' of compelled yet morally ambiguous choices"[110]. As Levi notes,

> the history of the Lagers has been written almost exclusively by those who, like myself, never fathomed them to the bottom. Those who did so did not return, or their capacity for observation was paralyzed by suffering and incomprehension.[111]

> We, the survivors, are not the true witnesses. [...] We survivors are not only an exiguous, but also an anomalous minority: we are those who by their prevarications or abilities or good luck did not touch bottom. Those who did so, those who saw the Gorgon, have not returned to tell about it or have returned mute; but they are the "Muslims", the submerged, the complete witnesses, the ones whose deposition would have a general significance.[112]

Traumatized testimonies are always characterized by a tension between the will to testify and the inability to communicate: the moral imperative to bear witness to the horrors of the Holocaust is haunted by the impossibility of narrating it. Survivors often claim that they cannot find the words to communicate their experience: "our language lacks words to express this offence, the demolition of a man"[113].

---

[108] D. Laub, "Truth and Testimony", p. 66.
[109] *Ibid.*, p. 65.
[110] G. Hartman, *Scars of the Spirit*, p. 86.
[111] P. Levi, *The Drowned and the Saved*, trans. R. Rosenthal, New York: Summit Books, 1988, p. 17. [Trans. from *I sommersi e i salvati*, Torino: Einaudi, 1986].
[112] *Ibid.*, pp. 83-84.
[113] P. Levi, *Survival in Auschwitz*, p. 26.

The victims' difficulty in narrating their traumatic experiences is mirrored by the outside world's difficulty in listening to them[114]. Hence, survivors struggle not only with memory and language, but also against reluctant listeners. Therefore, we should look for a mode of "listening and responding to traumatic stories in a way that does not lose their impact, that does not reduce them to clichés"[115].

The collapse of witnessing caused by the experience of the Holocaust is also a crisis of authenticity and truth: the longer a story remains untold, the more distorted it becomes[116]. However, the authenticity of a traumatic narrative does not depend on its accuracy. Language bears witness to trauma precisely through the failure of representation: paradoxically, it is when the referential function of words begins to break down that we can have a true testimony.

In "Education and Crisis", Shoshana Felman describes testimony as fragmented and broken in form,

> composed of bits and pieces of a memory that has been overwhelmed by occurrences that have not settled into understanding or remembrance, acts that cannot be constructed as knowledge nor assimilated into full cognition, events in excess of our frames of reference.[117]

Similarly, Langer claims that the plot of testimonies "meanders, coils back on itself, contains rocks and rapids, and requires strenuous effort to follow its intricate turns"[118]. However, the inarticulateness of trauma testimonies does not lead to meaninglessness: the gaps and disruptions bear witness to the authenticity and truth of trauma by showing that the traumatic experience has not been fully grasped. Testimony is thus a mode of realization of truth, and of access to authenticity.

In traumatized testimonies what is most significant is often what is left unsaid: fitting together the broken pieces of the testimony forces the reader or listener to look behind and beyond language. Faced with a fragmentary, non-linear narrative, the reader searches for connections between the "bits and pieces", in order to provide the unwritten part of the text. Therefore, the impossibility of a coherent trauma testimony does not only bear witness to the truth of trauma, but also favors an empathetic, ethical response: being actively

---

[114] See M. Humphrey, "From Terror to Trauma: Commissioning Truth for National Reconciliation", *Journal for Cultural Research* 6.1 (2000), p. 11.
[115] C. Caruth, "Preface", in C. Caruth (ed.), *Trauma: Explorations in Memory*, p. vii.
[116] See D. Laub, "Truth and Testimony", p. 64.
[117] S. Felman, "Education and Crisis", p. 16.
[118] L. Langer, *Holocaust Testimonies: The Ruins of Memory*, Yale: Yale University Press, 1991, p. 174.

engaged in the creation of meaning, the reader is more likely to be emotionally involved.

As we will see in Part II, this is precisely what happens in Martin Amis's novel *Time's Arrow*: while not belonging to the genre of testimony, Amis's novel reproduces the characteristics of traumatized testimonies on a formal level, by reversing the chronological order of the narrative, and questions the possibility of a truthful narrative, by presenting the events from the point of view of an unreliable narrator.

1.5 Trauma and history

Traditional historiography was bound up with notions of objectivity, reality and truth. It usually displayed a belief in realism, and considered historical representation as offering direct access to the reality of past events. Historical narrative was supposed to be a truthful story corresponding to the real events of the past, and its literary aspect was considered as a mere stylistic ornament. According to this view, historians were different from writers of fiction insofar as, while the latter invented everything in their narratives, historians invented nothing. In the last decades, however, an anxiety has developed "that nothing is what it appears to be, that everything, eventually, will turn out to be deceptive, manipulated, counterfeit" [119]. Therefore, "it should not come as a surprise that received historical fact is felt to be as fallible as any other"[120]. In fact, since the 1970s, the study of history has been influenced by a postmodern relativism that blurs the distinction between historical and fictional writing, and questions the possibility of objective historical knowledge.

According to postmodern theories of history, the historian's subjectivity necessarily informs representations of the past: since facts and interpretation cannot be clearly separated, a description of events inevitably conveys the historian's own interpretation. Moreover, meaning in history is subjective not only because it is constituted through acts of emplotment and interpretation, but also because the opaqueness of language affects it: the limits of language and narrative, as well as the limitations of the historian's individual perspective, influence historical representations. Therefore, historical objectivity is impossible: historians inescapably interpret, and thus shape, the history they want to document.

The relationships among facts are created by historians in literary and linguistic structures, that is, in plots and tropes. The narrativist thesis, according to which literary tropes and linguistic structures dominate history writing, has

---

[119] G. Hartman, *Scars of the Spirit*, p. 61.
[120] *Ibid.*

been mainly inspired by Hayden White[121]. As White points out, past events need to be *emplotted* in order to acquire historical meaning. Therefore, perfectly objective, universally true history cannot exist, because historical narratives always depend upon language and narratology: "there is an inexpungeable relativity in every representation of historical phenomena. Stories [...] are linguistic entities and belong to the order of discourse"[122].

Furthermore, historical events do not mandate any particular narrative treatment, because no meaning or interconnection is to be found in the facts themselves, which are "value-neutral"[123]. Plots are not immanent in events: historical situations are not intrinsically story-like, that is, they are neither inherently tragic nor comic[124]. Hence, historians can develop competing interpretations of the past, because any succession of real events can be emplotted in various ways: "when it comes to apprehending the historical record, there are no grounds to be found in the historical record itself for preferring one way of construing its meaning over another"[125].

According to Hayden White, historical narratives allow "alternative, mutually exclusive, and yet, equally plausible interpretations"[126] of the same set of events. However, it is important to underline that White is not arguing for a history that allows us to deny that events have taken place at all: his *epistemological* relativism does not lead to *moral* relativism, because he keeps the epistemology and the ethics of representation clearly separated, distinguishing between "a lie and an error or a mistake in interpretation"[127].

> [A]n interpretation falls into the category of a lie when it denies the reality of the events of which it treats, and into the category of an untruth when it draws false conclusions from reflection on events whose reality remains attestable on the level of positive historical inquiry.[128]

---

[121] See H. White, *Metahistory: The Historical Imagination in Nineteenth-Century Europe*, Baltimore, London: Johns Hopkins University Press, 1975.
[122] H. White, "Historical Emplotment and the Problem of Truth", in S. Friedländer, ed., *Probing the Limits of Representation: Nazism and the "Final Solution"*, Cambridge, Mass.: Harvard University Press, 1992, p. 37.
[123] H. White, "The Historical Text as Literary Artifact", in H. White, *Tropics of Discourse: Essays in Cultural Criticism*, Baltimore, London: Johns Hopkins University Press, 1985, p. 85.
[124] H. White, "The Question of Narrative in Contemporary Historical Theory", in H. White, *The Content of the Form: Narrative Discourse and Historical Representation*, Baltimore, London: Johns Hopkins University Press, 1987, p. 44.
[125] H. White, "The Politics of Historical Interpretation: Discipline and De-Sublimation", in *The Content of the Form*, p. 75.
[126] H. White, "The Historical Text as Literary Artifact", p. 93.
[127] H. White, "The Politics of Historical Interpretation", p. 77.
[128] *Ibid.*, p. 78.

White avoids falling into absolute relativism by arguing that, although closeness to reality cannot be measured according to universal criteria, nor proven scientifically, historical narratives can nonetheless be evaluated case by case, and assessed in terms of truth value:

> Considered as accounts of events already established as facts, "competing narratives" can be assessed, criticized, and ranked on the basis of their fidelity to the factual record, their comprehensiveness, and the coherence of whatever arguments they may contain.[129]

Postmodern theories about the narrative construction of reality have revealed that the relationship between facts and their representation is problematic: representation *constructs* reality rather than *mirroring* it. The writing of history thus implies the creation of a substitute for reality: as there is no direct link between the past and its historiographic representation, the form in which historical events are presented is necessarily constructed by the historian. Accordingly, postmodern historiography questions the existence of a direct connection between representation and reality, and claims that there is no unmediated access to the facts of history: facts are shaped by the discursive forms in which they are emplotted.

Moreover, the postmodernist aestheticizing of history, that is, its assimilation into the literary and aesthetic domain, blurs the distinctions between facts and fiction: literature and history are similar insofar as they are both constituted as textualized thought and are thus subject to the limits of language and writing. In the same way as authors of fictional narratives, historians shape the facts by means of language and rhetoric, and emplot them according to one of the main literary genres (epic, romance, tragedy, comedy, or farce)[130].

In 1967 Roland Barthes first challenged the distinction between historical and fictional discourse by asking:

> Does the narration of past events, which, in our culture from the time of the Greeks onwards, has generally been subject to the sanction of historical 'science', bound to the unbending standard of the 'real', and justified by the principles of 'rational' exposition - does this form of narration really differ, in some specific trait, in some indubitably distinctive feature, from imaginary narration, as we find it in the epic, the novel, and the drama?[131]

Hayden White's reconceptualization of the relationship between factual and fictional narratives merges fiction and history writing by claiming that they

---

[129] H. White, "Historical Emplotment and the Problem of Truth", p. 38.
[130] H. White, "The Question of Narrative in Contemporary Historical Theory", p. 43.
[131] R. Barthes, "The Discourse of History", *Comparative Criticism* 3 (1981), p. 7.

entail the same representational strategies. The emplotment of historical events in a meaningful story, with a beginning, middle and end, does not correspond to the actual and factual reality of the past: historians constantly make up stories in order to transform a meaningless succession of events into a coherent narrative. Thus, narrativity is not only a mere vehicle for conveying information – a tactic that historians may or may not use – but a necessary means for symbolizing events.

History and literature are thus not diametrically opposed. Instead, they are very similar, as they both have a verbal structure: historians and novelists employ the same linguistic and rhetorical structures and strategies. Hence, there is a stylistic dimension in historical writing, and the distinction between form and content can no longer be taken for granted: in the postmodern era, historians need to recognize the aesthetic nature of historiography.

White's narrative approach to the writing of history aims at aestheticizing history and dismantling its foundations in ideas of truth and reality, moving towards a poststructuralist textualism. His claim that history is "infinitely interpretable and ultimately undecidable"[132] might lead to the assumption that in reading history we are reading merely fictive stories. However, White does not argue that history must be regarded as fiction, nor that historical narratives dispel false beliefs about the past: in fact, inherent in his idea of historical narrative there is always an "impulse to moralize reality"[133].

As we have seen, according to traditional historiography, the narrative form does not add anything to the content of the representation. On the contrary, postmodern historiography claims that the narrative dimension of history is not a mere decoration, but contributes to the very *creation* of the facts: it is precisely the narrative structure in which facts are embedded that endows them with meaning. Therefore, form matters: "it is the choice of the story type and its imposition upon the events that endow them with meaning"[134] and provide an illusory coherence and significance to otherwise meaningless facts.

Historical meaning cannot be transparent also because the dynamics of meaning production depend on the relation between texts and contexts. As Dominick LaCapra underlines, "[n]o text entirely transcends an uncritical implication in contemporary ideologies and prejudices"[135]. Similarly, Roland Barthes argues that "historical discourse is in its essence a form of ideological elaboration"[136]. In fact, historical knowledge is always mediated by some form of repression or exclusion: narrative is not merely a neutral and transparent

---

[132] H. White, "Historical Emplotment and the Problem of Truth", p. 38.
[133] H. White, "The Value of Narrativity in the Representation of Reality", in *The Content of the Form*, p. 14.
[134] H. White, "The Question of Narrative in Contemporary Historical Theory", p. 44.
[135] D. LaCapra, *Representing the Holocaust*, p. 25.
[136] R. Barthes, "The Discourse of History", p. 16.

medium for the representation of historical events, but has ideological and political implications. Furthermore, according to White,

> while it is possible to produce a kind of knowledge that is not explicitly linked to any specific political program, all knowledge produced in the human and social sciences lends itself to use by a given ideology better than it does to others.[137]

This has led many historians to reject aspirations of objectivity in favour of an "ethic of fairness". White also argues that the fictionalization of history and its assimilation to literature "in no way detracts from the status as knowledge which we ascribe to historiography"[138], because also literature, being a product of this world, teaches us something about reality:

> If historians were to recognize the fictive element in their narratives, this would not mean the degradation of historiography to the status of ideology or propaganda. In fact, this recognition would serve as an antidote to the tendency of historians to become captive of ideological preconceptions which they [...] honor as the "correct" perception of "the way things *really* are". By drawing historiography nearer to its origin in literary sensibility, we should be able to identify the ideological, because it is the fictive, element in our own discourse.[139]

1.6 Representing the Holocaust

The Holocaust is often perceived as a *Nullpunkt* in history, a "point zero" from which history could begin again. It is an event that challenges the traditional patterns of historical representation, a trauma so extreme as to unsettle or even annihilate the categories and standards of judgement by which we evaluate things. Jean-François Lyotard expresses this idea through the metaphor of an earthquake that destroys all instruments of measurement:

> Suppose that an earthquake destroys not only lives, buildings, and objects but also the instruments used to measure earthquakes directly and indirectly. The impossibility of quantitatively measuring it does not prohibit, but rather inspires in the minds of the survivors the idea of a very great seismic force.[140]

---

[137] H. White, "The Politics of Historical Interpretation", p. 81.
[138] H. White, "The Historical Text as Literary Artifact", p. 99.
[139] *Ibid.*
[140] J. F. Lyotard, *The Differend: Phrases in Dispute*, trans. G. Van Den Abbeele, Minneapolis: University of Columbia Press, 1990, p. 56.

Similarly, the difficulties inherent in describing the Holocaust, its inconceivability and unimaginability, and the impossibility of interpreting it according to our traditional patterns of understanding are linked to the fact that such an extreme, traumatic event destroys the instruments we need in order to comprehend it within our mental schemes.

The historical narrativization of the Holocaust raises not only aesthetic problems, but also moral issues. In particular, it poses questions about the ethics of historical representation: are there any limits on the possibilities of emplotment for writing histories about Auschwitz? According to Hayden White, "[t]here is an inexpungeable relativity in every representation of historical phenomena"[141], and any event can be emplotted in a number of ways without violating established historical facts. However, White makes an exception when it comes to traumatic limit events such as the Holocaust: for him, the possibilities of emplotment of the Holocaust are limited by what is currently considered an acceptable mode of interpretation.

The question of the limits of representation of the Nazi genocide is a relevant issue in history writing, and the problem of Holocaust representation is often considered as different in degree from that of other events, as there are ethical values which draw a line between acceptable and unacceptable emplotments. Therefore, the Holocaust – and, more generally, traumatic events – allow for less flexibility of representation than ordinary events. They demand to pose ethical limits upon relativism in order to be able to discern right and wrong, truth and falsity: for example, denying the Holocaust is both immoral and empirically wrong.

However, there are no absolute limits on the kind of emplotments that can be imposed upon the events of the Holocaust. Some emplotments might be regarded as inappropriate, because they seem to violate "certain rules of decorum"[142], but historical facts themselves do not possess a particular story-form: hence, we cannot determine whether a historical account succeeds or fails on the basis of the emplotment's "adherence" to the facts. For example, although a comic or pastoral emplotment of the history of the Third Reich could be dismissed from the list of competing narratives by claiming that it is not faithful to the facts, because there is nothing comic or pastoral about the Holocaust, such an emplotment would be a fruitful representation of the Holocaust if the narration was presented in a pointedly ironic way, to poke fun at narratives of the Third Reich emplotted in the mode of comic or pastoral[143]. In this sense, White praises Art Spiegelman's comic treatment of Auschwitz in *Maus: A*

---

[141] H. White, "Historical Emplotment and the Problem of Truth", p. 37.
[142] J. E. Young, "Toward a Received History of the Holocaust", *History and Theory* 36.4 (1997), p. 26.
[143] H. White, "Historical Emplotment and the Problem of Truth, p. 40.

Survivor's Tale[144], because, he argues, "it makes the difficulty of discovering and telling the whole truth about even a small part of [the Holocaust] as much a part of the story as the events whose meaning it is seeking to discover"[145].

Therefore, I think that all kinds of narrative emplotments, linguistic tropes and stylistic treatments could be adopted in the representation of the Holocaust. Yet, not all representations are equal in quality, and certain approaches are indeed more appropriate than others: pluralism does not mean acritical relativism, and it is indeed possible to judge historical representations according to their ethical and truth value. On an ethical level, there are unacceptable modes of emplotment for representing Nazi history: in particular, as Hayden White denounces, the denial of the Holocaust is "as morally offensive as it is intellectually bewildering"[146]. Hence, White's ethical concern "to defend certain meanings and, consequently, to police representations that violate one's normative system"[147] and moral values makes it impossible to say that a Nazi interpretation of the Holocaust or its denial are as valid as any other interpretation.

Representing the Holocaust requires not only a rethinking of the ethics of historical representation, but also new categories of analysis, a new language, and new narrative strategies. The traumatic character of the Holocaust poses special demands on its historical representation, because it can only be communicated through a refusal of the traditional frameworks of understanding. In particular, realism as a means of historical representation has to be dismissed. Accordingly, Dominick LaCapra argues that historians need to rethink traditional categories when they are confronted with traumatic events, also questioning any positivist approach to history: "the study of the Holocaust may help us to reconsider the requirements of historiography in general. Conventional techniques are particularly inadequate with respect to events that are indeed limiting"[148].

According to LaCapra, trying to represent extremely traumatic events may cause language to break down: "Auschwitz [...] is the extreme limit case that threatens classifications, categories, and comparisons. It may reduce one to silence."[149] However, he does not regard the silence caused by trauma as

---

[144] A. Spiegelman, *Maus: A Survivor's Tale*, New York: Pantheon Books, 1993. In this two-volumes set of comics, Spiegelman narrates the story of his father Vladek, a Holocaust survivor. The peculiarity of Spiegelman's representation is that the human characters are depicted as animals: the Jews as mice, the Germans as cats, and the Americans as dogs.
[145] H. White, "Historical Emplotment and the Problem of Truth", p. 41.
[146] H. White, "The Politics of Historical Interpretation", p. 76.
[147] J. Varon, "Probing the Limits of the Politics of Representation", *New German Critique* 72 (1997), p. 95.
[148] D. LaCapra, *Representing the Holocaust*, pp. 46-7.
[149] *Ibid.*, p. 65.

equivalent to complete muteness: for him, "the way language breaks down is itself a significant and even telling process"[150].

LaCapra also notes how the Holocaust is often perceived as "a traumatic point of rupture between modernism and post-modernism. In this light, the postmodern and the post-Holocaust become mutually intertwined issues that are best addressed in relation to each other"[151]. Postmodern literature and theory represent a reaction to the traumas of the twentieth century, and to the resulting moral upheaval. Hence, the issues raised by postmodern historiography, such as the impossibility of historical objectivity, the question of truth, the limits of narrativity and language, the role of the historian in shaping historical narratives, the critique of totalization, are inextricably linked to Holocaust and Trauma Studies.

In Holocaust and Trauma Studies, the question of representation has always been characterized by a tension between a resistance to closure and a need for communication. Indeed, the Shoah calls for a mode of representation that does not suppress its traumatic nature by constraining it within a coherently structured narrative form: since the trauma of the Holocaust goes beyond any human power of verbalization and conceptualization, it takes a traumatic and traumatized narrative, that is, a story that remains within trauma, characterized by fragmentation and lack of closure, to represent it adequately.

According to Hayden White, the Holocaust is an exemplary modern event. Hence, its representation requires an emblematically modern style of narrative: "modernist modes of representation may offer possibilities of representing the reality of both the Holocaust and the experience of it that no other version of realism could do"[152]. White follows Berel Lang in suggesting that "intransitive writing" and "middle-voicedness" are the most suitable techniques for representing the Holocaust. Lang, and consequently White, conceive intransitive writing as a fusion of writer, text, and reader into the writing act. In intransitive writing, an author "writes himself' [...]. Writing becomes itself the means of comprehension, not a mirror of something independent, but an act and a commitment – a doing or making rather than a reflection or a description"[153].

The middle voice is a third possibility of diathesis that exists in some languages (for example, in ancient Greek) in addition to the active and the passive voice, and it expresses a peculiar relation between agent and action: "[w]hereas in the active and passive voices the subject of the verb is presumed to be external to the action, as either agent or patient, in the middle voice the

---

[150] *Ibid.*, p. 47.
[151] *Ibid.*, p. 188.
[152] H. White, "Historical Emplotment and the Problem of Truth", p. 52.
[153] B. Lang, *Act and Idea in the Nazi Genocide*, Chicago: University of Chicago Press, 1990, p. xii.

subject is presumed to be *interior* to the action"[154]. Following Barthes, White claims that in literary modernism "the verb 'to write' connotes neither an active nor a passive relationship, but rather a middle one"[155]. The fusion of writer, text, and reader typical of the modernist style is linked to the fact that "in the middle voice of *to write,* the distance between scriptor and language diminishes asymptotically"[156]. Hence, the middle voice can be considered as an adequate technique for representing trauma, insofar as it does not appear as "a vehicle for truth claims or for ethico-political judgments having any significant degree of decisiveness"[157], but problematizes any claim and judgment, indicating a sense of ambiguity, uncertainty, and openness. Accordingly, Saul Friedländer calls for the introduction of the historian's voice into historical narratives of the Holocaust[158].

The experimental forms of postmodern fiction represent a fruitful means for representing the shocking force of trauma, insofar as they create self-conscious narratives that recognize their own limitations and the impossibility of finding definitive answers. The representation of the Holocaust, both in history and in fiction, is characterized by a refusal of narrative closure that may confuse and overwhelm the reader, but at the same time help him or her empathizing with the victims' traumatic past.

Saul Friedländer insists on the necessity of narrative disruption in Holocaust representations, claiming that the risk of closure inherent in the linear progression of narrative might lead to an avoidance of what in history remains "indeterminate, elusive, and opaque"[159]. On the contrary, narrative disruption enables the historian to register, and thus the reader to perceive, the opaqueness and indecipherability of trauma[160].

Similarly, Cathy Caruth argues that too coherent a narrative of trauma may cause a loss of its shocking force and distort its reality: the integration of trauma within a well-structured, organized narrative "may lose both the precision and the force that characterizes traumatic recall"[161]. Therefore, Caruth proposes a performative theory according to which, in order to truthfully transmit the impact of trauma to others, the traumatic event cannot be narrated, but only *performed* in its literariness, as if it were happening all over again.

---

[154] *Ibid.,* p. 48.
[155] *Ibid.*
[156] R. Barthes, "To Write: An Intransitive Verb?", in R. Barthes, *The Rustle of Language,* trans. R. Howard, Berkley: University of California Press, 1989, p. 19.
[157] D. LaCapra, *Writing,* p. 197.
[158] S. Friedländer, "Introduction", in *Probing the Limits of Representation,* p. 17.
[159] S. Friedländer, "Introduction", p. 3.
[160] *Ibid.,* p. 5.
[161] C. Caruth, "Recapturing the Past", p. 153.

For Caruth, since trauma is an incomprehensible event that defies all representation, a coherent narrative risks not only loosing the precision of trauma, but also betraying "the *truth of an event*, and the *truth of its incomprehensibility* [...], the force of its *affront to understanding*"[162]. In my opinion, the theory of trauma proposed by Caruth provides an ethical solution to the crisis of representation posed by trauma: by preserving the truth of trauma in its literariness, and transmitting it to others in a traumatic and traumatized account, the performative representation of trauma sets upon readers an ethical obligation to empathize with the victims and share their sufferings.

1.7 Trauma as a pathology of history

According to Cathy Caruth, trauma "is not a pathology [...] of falsehood or displacement of meaning, but of history itself"[163]:

> If PTSD must be understood as a pathological symptom, then it is not so much a symptom of the unconscious, as it is a symptom of history. The traumatized, we might say, carry an impossible history within them, or they become themselves the symptom of a history that they cannot entirely possess.[164]

History is a history of trauma because, like trauma, it is not fully perceived as it occurs, but it becomes meaningful only belatedly. The inherent latency within the experience of trauma reflects the belated temporal structure of historical experience: "For history to be a history of trauma means that [...] a history can be grasped only in the very inaccessibility of its occurrence"[165].

The re-enactments of the past that characterize traumatic experiences bear witness to a history that was not fully experienced at the time of its occurrence. The traumatic nature of history has implications for the ways we represent it: on the one hand, trauma demands historical awareness and integration, but, on the other, it disrupts our usual modes of historical representation, resisting fixed narrative structures and linear temporalities.

A history of trauma perpetually escapes our understanding. Hence, the question that we should ask, and that remains without a definitive answer, is: "[h]ow is it possible [...] to gain access to a traumatic history?"[166]. If we consider history as inherently traumatic, we have to acknowledge the necessity

---

[162] C. Caruth, "Recapturing the Past", pp. 153-4.
[163] C. Caruth, "Trauma and Experience", p. 5.
[164] *Ibid.*
[165] *Ibid.*, p. 8.
[166] C. Caruth, "Recapturing the Past", p. 151.

of a history that is not straightforwardly referential, objective, and coherent, but fragmentary and disrupted, characterized by uncertainties and doubts, that is, we have to adopt a postmodernist view of historiography. According to this view, the historian does not aim at integration and totality: like the psychoanalyst, he or she must pay attention to what is not said, and focus on the historical scraps, the minor and seemingly irrelevant details that reveal what is suppressed. Hence, in a traumatic history "the essence of the past is not, or does not lie in, the essence of the past. It is the scraps, the slips of the tongue, the *Fehlleistungen* of the past, the rare moments when the past 'let[s] itself go'"[167].

Trauma is thus a crisis of history that causes conventional epistemologies to falter: it unsettles temporal structures and challenges the notion of a straightforward textual referentiality. The disrupted chronology that characterizes both historical and fictional narratives of trauma represents the unresolved nature of the past, the haunting quality of a traumatic history that has not been assimilated at the time of its occurrence. It is precisely the failure of a coherent narrative that allows traumatic history to be performatively constituted as such. Through the notion of trauma, we can understand that rethinking the categories of historical representation does not mean eliminating history, but resituating it in our understanding. Moreover, Caruth argues that traumatic history can only be communicated through a "contagion" of the listener. Hence, if history is a symptom of trauma, it is a symptom which must not be cured but simply transmitted.

The catastrophic condition we are experiencing has destabilized the traditional relation between history and representation, but, at the same time, "[i]n a catastrophic age [...] trauma itself may provide the very link between cultures"[168]: the experience of historical trauma might be the common denominator that keeps together all those who are living in the post-Holocaust era. In particular, Caruth quotes Freud's history of the Jews in *Moses and Monotheism* to underline how Jewish culture has been shaped by trauma: the repeated confrontation with anti-Semitism constitutes the very link uniting the Jewish nation[169].

Geoffrey Hartman seems to agree with Caruth's view of history as a history of trauma when he reverses Hegel's claim that "[t]he wounds made by the spirit leave no scars" by arguing that "[t]he spirit does leave scars [...] both evident and eloquent"[170]: those scars could be identified collectively with the "uncertain moral progress"[171] of history. In fact, according to Hartman,

---

[167] F. R. Ankersmit, "Historiography and Postmodernism", *History and Theory* 28.2 (1989), p. 148.
[168] C. Caruth, "Trauma and Experience", p. 11.
[169] C. Caruth, *Unclaimed Experience*, pp. 12-16.
[170] G. Hartman, *Scars of the Spirit*, p. 41.
[171] *Ibid.*

the vastness of Hegel's totalizing perspective does not succeed in envisioning history as a necessary and justified scene in which the agency of spirit leaves no scars. The scar, the traumatic or ecstatic memory trace, is never entirely erased and so becomes, whether we like it or not, the foundation of our sense of reality.[172]

Hence, for Hartman history is "not the story of human liberation but one wounding after another, a narrative of scars left in the wake of spiritual violence"[173].

The question of truth
The question of truth is relevant to the writing of any history but becomes crucial in the writing of a traumatic history such as that of the Holocaust. In fact, historians of the Holocaust have been particularly disquieted by the postmodern understanding of history, according to which historical narratives are subject to the limits of tropes and plots, and thus cannot objectively represent the reality of the past. The postmodern rejection of the possibility of identifying a stable truth challenges the need of Holocaust historians to ascertain the reality and truth of the Holocaust: according to postmodernist historians, the opaqueness and polysemy of language makes it impossible to satisfy the need for truth. For Lyotard, it is precisely in the attempt to write a truthful history of the Holocaust that the impossibility of a single, integrated historical narrative emerges[174]: since the voices of the perpetrators and those of the victims appear as mutually exclusive, any totalizing view of history is revealed as deceiving.

In Holocaust Studies, there has been a fear that considering historical facts as emplottable in a number of different ways might lead to an absolute relativism that allows any manipulation of historical facts, considering even a revisionist historical narrative that denies the Holocaust as an acceptable version of history. However, asserting the impossibility of historical objectivity and the difficulty of gaining access to a comprehensible story does not mean denying the possibility of a transmissible truth: the reality of traumatic history *can* be communicated if traditional modes of representation are dismissed in favour of fragmentary, inassimilable, and chronologically disrupted forms.

As Hayden White makes clear, the nature of the Holocaust is not merely a matter of opinion and, even if historical objectivity is not possible, historians still have a moral and social responsibility to "tell the truth"[175]. Therefore, postmodernism does not free historians from their ethical duties: they owe historical truth both to the living and to the dead.

---

[172] *Ibid.*, p. 43.
[173] *Ibid.*, p. 52.
[174] J. F. Lyotard, *The Differend*, pp. 56-7.
[175] H. White, "The Politics of Historical Interpretation", p. 76.

2. MARTIN AMIS'S *TIME'S ARROW* AS TRAUMA FICTION

2.1 Some preliminary considerations on art, ethics and language

Since Plato's *Republic* (390-387 BC), the relation between art and ethics has been at the forefront of Western thought. In Plato's dialogue, Socrates challenges poetry to demonstrate its right to exist in the ideal state: poetry should prove not only to be pleasant, but also to be useful to the State. Plato takes for granted the primacy of politics, and insists that art be subject to political control: the rulers of the state have a responsibility to recognize and control the ethical function of art. The right of the poets to a place in the Republic is questioned on the basis that, by shaping the self-understanding of the citizens, they usurp the role of the educators.

According to Plato, art should guide and enlighten existence, convey illuminating truths, and emphasize what is good in men, that is, it should perform an ethical function. Since he considers it irresponsible to entrust the power of shaping the ethos to someone who may not satisfy the demands of morality, Plato banishes artists from the ideal Republic, and insists that art be controlled by the state rulers, who know what is in the state's best interest.

In contemporary thought, the relation between art and ethics is perceived as more flexible, and it has even been denied in the name of the artist's power: as Berel Lang notes, "the undoubted power of art and the artist" has sustained the view according to which "art transcends the expressive forms of ethics"[176]. However, the artist has indeed an ethical responsibility. The ethical relevance of literature is given by the fact that it expresses contradictions between different values and presents us with diversity and otherness without reducing them to unity, thereby favouring an ethics of free pluralism[177]. Literature thus requires a responsible, moral, and spiritual approach.

In "The Ethical Criticism of Art", Berys Gaut proposes a strong argument for ethicism by claiming that the ethical evaluation of a work of art "is a legitimate aspect of the aesthetic evaluation"[178], so that "if a work manifests ethically reprehensible attitudes, it is to that extent aesthetically defective, and if a work manifests ethically commendable attitudes, it is to that extent aesthetically meritorious"[179]. However, there have been objections to Gaut's view on the basis that there are indeed "good but evil works [...] and poor but virtuous

---

[176] B. Lang, *Holocaust Representation: Art Within the Limits of History and Ethics*, Baltimore, London: Johns Hopkins University Press, 2000, p. 4.
[177] A. Gibson, *Postmodernity, Ethics and the Novel*, London, New York: Routledge, 1999, p. 8.
[178] B. Gaut, "The Ethical Criticism of Art", in J. Levinson, ed., *Aesthetics and Ethics: Essays at the Intersection*, Cambridge: Cambridge University Press, 1998, p. 182.
[179] *Ibid.*

works"[180]. Similarly, Noël Carroll holds that a moral defect in a work of art may count as an aesthetic one and a moral virtue as an aesthetic virtue[181], but he moderates Gaut's moralism by arguing that a work of art cannot change our moral outlook, although it may "stretch and deepen our moral understanding"[182].

In order to clarify the "tumultuous relationship" between art and morality, Todorov identifies three theories about this relation: "the first, that suggests poetry should bow to morality; the second, that would have morality yield to poetry; and the last, which affirms that the two domains ought to remain separate and independent"[183].

The first theory, which he calls "classical", considers art in the service of moral principles, and argues that aesthetic values should be subjected to ethical ones: as we have seen, this is the position expressed by Plato. According to the second theory, defined by Todorov as "romantic", poetry should have the privilege over morality, and art the privilege over life. Such a replacement of ethical values by aesthetic ones has been attempted by twentieth-century regimes:

> Think of the exaltation of the big, blond Aryan opposed to the small, dark Jew; or of the role of the spectacular staging of public meetings, or of the monumental architecture of the pre-war years; or of the fact that Communist totalitarianism, despite its predilection for ideology, cultivated grand spectacle and was in no way indifferent to the aesthetic dimension of public life.[184]

Todorov also highlights how even contemporary, democratic societies are characterized by an attempt to substitute ethics with aesthetics: "our current democratic societies display the particular perversion of transforming political debate into spectacle, which in the end also implies that aesthetic considerations triumph over moral and political questions"[185].

Finally, the third theory identified by Todorov asserts the autonomy of aesthetic and ethical values. This is the theory he personally advocates: "[t]he beauty of works of art insures neither their morality, nor their political rightness [...] On the other hand, countless examples demonstrate that good ethical values are not enough to produce a good poem"[186].

---

[180] O. Conolly, "Review", p. 394.
[181] N. Carroll, "Moderate Moralism", *British Journal of Aesthetics* 36.3 (1996), p. 234.
[182] N. Carroll, "Art, Narrative, and Moral Understanding", in J. Levinson, ed., *Aesthetics and Ethics*, p. 149.
[183] T. Todorov, "Poetry and Morality", *Salmagundi* 111 (1996), p. 69.
[184] *Ibid.*, pp. 70-1.
[185] *Ibid.*, p. 71.
[186] *Ibid.*

However, Todorov recognizes that it is necessary to place certain limitations on the separation of the two domains. In fact, he thinks that poets accomplish their moral duty by producing beautiful, meaningful work: poetry contributes to improving the world by adding beauty to it, and by making it more intelligible and richer in meaning. According to Todorov, "what we expect from the greatest creators is [...] the capacity for understanding and for making us understand even the most horrible acts, the most inhuman designs."[187]

The ethics of Holocaust representation

After the Holocaust, the quarrel between ethics and aesthetics has acquired great significance. The trauma of the Holocaust has disrupted traditional moral frameworks, so that the conventional ethical values that had previously guided social life had to be reconsidered. Representing the Holocaust raises ethical issues more significant than those posed by the representation of "ordinary" historical events. Since Adorno's claim that "to write poetry after Auschwitz is barbaric"[188], it has even been questioned whether *any* aestheticizing of the Holocaust is morally acceptable.

In several works, philosopher Berel Lang has explored the general moral relevance of the Holocaust, arguing that the Holocaust is so atrocious that it is incomprehensible and unrepresentable[189]. According to Lang, there are ethical and historical limits impinging on Holocaust representations, and the ideal of historical authenticity should be present even in openly imaginative Holocaust narratives[190].

Geoffrey Hartman, observing how contemporary art has almost total freedom of expression, argues: "even in the case of the Shoah there are no limits of representation, only limits of conceptualization"[191]. Indeed, the main difficulty is interpreting what happens: "when domination and terror become absolutes, that is, when they are *ideologized* and *totalized*, [...] we cannot discover in ourselves a possible scenario to explain what happened"[192].

According to Hartman, dealing with extreme trauma requires extreme representational means, because "a massive realism [...] not only desensitizes but produces the opposite of what is intended: an *unreality effect* that fatally undermines realism's claim to depict reality"[193]. Holocaust narratives always

---

[187] *Ibid.*
[188] T. Adorno, *Prisms*, trans. Samuel and Shierry Weber, Cambridge: MIT Press, 1997, p. 34.
[189] See B. Lang, *Act and Idea in the Nazi Genocide*; *Holocaust Representation*; *The Future of the Holocaust: Between History and Memory*, New York: Cornell University Press, 1999; *Writing and the Holocaust*, New York, London: Holmes and Meier, 1988.
[190] B. Lang, *Holocaust Representation*, p. xii.
[191] G. Hartman, *The Longest Shadow*, p. 118.
[192] *Ibid.*, p. 120.
[193] *Ibid.*, p. 157.

require an ethical response: more than any other genre, Holocaust literature poses the ethical question of responsibility. Therefore, not only writers but also readers have an ethical responsibility towards Holocaust texts: while empathy cannot relieve suffering, an ethically engaged interpretation makes it possible to respond appropriately to narratives of trauma.

As Sara Horowitz has underlined, "the conjunction of fiction with the historical events of the Holocaust has made both readers and writers uneasy"[194], and it has also troubled critics and philosophers: "there is a high degree of discomfort with the idea of an aesthetic project built upon actual atrocity"[195]. Horowitz further notes the contradiction that resides at the very heart of Holocaust representation: the idea that it is impossible to express such a traumatic experience is challenged by a moral obligation to do so, and the claims of unspeakability and unrepresentability of the Holocaust are unsettled by the existence of several works that actually represent it.

One of the most challenging questions raised by Holocaust fiction is whether a postmodern style is an ethically appropriate response to extreme experience. Martin Amis's postmodern novel *Time's Arrow* destabilizes our conception of what is appropriate in relation to Holocaust representation: is the mode of tragedy the only proper means of representing the catastrophe? Or are humor and irony ethically acceptable?

As I will try to illustrate, I think that considering *Time's Arrow* unethical is absolutely pointless: every structural and stylistic device in this novel – from the time's reversal to the unreliable narrator, from humor in the first part of the novel to dark irony in the Auschwitz section – everything has a moral purpose and aims at Amis's ultimate goal, which is to overcome the indifference and desensitization caused by routine exposure to images of trauma and violence.

Through its style, *Time's Arrow* makes self-reflection, moral reckoning, and social action necessary for readers, who are forced to move beyond the aesthetic value of the novel to examine their own potential complicity in evil. The reader is drawn in, spellbound by the contradictions: Amis places us in what Levi calls "the gray zone"[196], so that we dwell in the midst of moral uncertainty and ambiguity.

Some critics have questioned the ethics of aestheticizing trauma. However, I think that the aesthetics of Amis's novel can have an ethical function: by shocking us, it brings us to understand the horror of trauma, and thus it may help us prevent such events from occurring again. As Iris Murdoch has claimed, art is able to penetrate the consciousness of the reader in ways that other means are

---

[194] S. Horowitz, *Voicing the Void: Muteness and Memory in Holocaust Fiction*, Albany: State University of New York Press, 1997, p. 15.
[195] *Ibid.*, p. 8.
[196] P. Levi, *The Drowned and the Saved*, p. 36.

unable to do: "Art transcends selfish and obsessive limitations of personality and can enlarge the sensibility of its consumer. It is a kind of goodness by proxy"[197]. As trauma shatters one's world view in a negative way, art and beauty alter it in a constructive way. Hence, the beauty of trauma fiction does not work *against* the shocking force of trauma: instead, it amplifies its effect upon the reader. The power of great literature lays precisely in its ability to leave the audience transformed, which is exactly what *Time's Arrow* does: the encounter with Amis's novel has indeed a strong impact on an attentive reader.

The role of language

> In its original form, when it was given to men by God himself, language was an absolutely certain and transparent sign for things, because it resembled them. [...] This transparency was destroyed at Babel as a punishment for men. Languages became separated and incompatible with one another only in so far as they had previously lost this original resemblance to the things that had been the prime reason for the existence of language. [...] But though language no longer bears an immediate resemblance to the things it names, this does not mean that it is separate from the world; it still continues, in another form, to be the locus of revelations and to be included in the area where truth is both manifested and expressed.[198]

As Foucault notes, while the transparency of language was destroyed after Babel, the idea of a relation between language and reality continued to be valued until the modern period, both with the romantic emphasis on language and nature as the media of divine revelation and with the structuralist focus on the relation between signifier and signified.

In "The Resistance to Theory", Paul De Man questions the traditional assumption that language refers to the material world, proposing a "literary" understanding of the relationship between words and things, according to which language refers only to itself[199]. De Man's claim that "the relationship between word and thing is not phenomenal but conventional"[200] derives from De Saussure's structuralist theory, which underlines how language cannot be directly and mimetically linked to reality, because signification is arbitrary[201].

---

[197] I. Murdoch, "The Sovereignty of Good Over Other Concepts", in I. Murdoch, *Existentialists and Mystics: Writings on Philosophy and Literature*, New York: Penguin Books, 1999, p. 371.
[198] M. Foucault, *The Order of Things: An Archaeology of Human Sciences*, New York: Vintage, 1994, p. 36.
[199] P. De Man, "The Resistance to Theory", in P. De Man, *The Resistance to Theory*, Minneapolis: University of Minnesota Press, 1986, p. 9.
[200] *Ibid.*, p. 10.
[201] F. De Saussure, *Course in General Linguistics,* trans. R. Harris, Chicago: Open Court, 1986.

According to De Man, language resists the fixing of meaning that mimetic representation seeks to achieve, because it is uncertain and volatile[202]. He thus dismisses the assumption that language *reflects* reality, proposing instead that language *constitutes* reality: we know *through* language. By undermining the authority of language as a mimetic tool, De Man questions the authority of any linguistic construction of history, and in so doing he reveals the constructedness of the binary opposition "fiction versus reality": everything is fiction because everything is language. Hence, the poststructuralist development of Saussure's structuralism has consequences also for the study of history and literature.

The notion of language as the ultimate foundation of reality refers back to Kant's "Copernican Revolution", according to which it is language that makes the object possible and creates reality, not the other way round[203]. Kant rejects the belief that meaning is correlated with an external, objective reality, and argues that we cannot reach a direct knowledge of the object, unmediated by language: knowledge is language-based, and truth is internal to representation. Our inability to escape representation renders the "thing-in-itself" (*Ding an sich*) unattainable[204]. Later on, with the advent of modern linguistic theory (in particular De Saussure's structuralism and De Man's post-structuralism), this idea began to be expressed in terms of the arbitrariness of the linguistic sign.

No less than the object, also the subject is founded in language: identity is constructed in and through language. As Heidegger notes, our alienation from being stems from our estrangement from language[205]: through the human manipulation and mishandling of the essence of language, we have lost our way on the path to thinking and being, and to the true essence of language.

The relevance of modern linguistic theories to Trauma Studies is given by the fact that trauma, by causing a breakdown of language, disrupts the survivor's identity and attacks the very meaning of one's life. In fact, we are unable to approach memory through anything except language: experience requires language to mediate reality, and it only gains meaning and becomes intelligible within language, when it has been spoken or written. Since trauma cannot be fully grasped by language, there is necessarily a gap between words and traumatic memory. The disruptions of Martin Amis's trauma novel *Time's Arrow* point precisely to this failure of language to fully comprehend a post-traumatic reality.

---

[202] P. De Man, "The Resistance to Theory", p. 10.
[203] T. Mautner, ed., *The Penguin Dictionary of Philosophy*, New York: Penguin Books, 1997, p. 291.
[204] I. Kant, *Critique of Pure Reason*, trans. P. Guyer and A. Wood, Cambridge: Cambridge University Press, 1998, p. 189.
[205] M. Heidegger, *Introduction to Metaphysics*, trans. G. Fried and R. Polt, New Haven, London: Yale University Press, 2000, p. 67. See also: M. Heidegger, *On the Way to Language*, trans. P. Hertz, New York: Harper, 1982.

Language and the Holocaust

The paradox of language in the post-Holocaust era could be described in terms of "simultaneous deficit and excess: language does less than we want and more than we intend"[206]. That is, language is deficient with respect to reference, while its effects of readability appear unlimited because subject to infinite interpretations[207]. In order to come to terms with the disruptions of language caused by the experience of the Holocaust, it is necessary to develop a new, postmodern language that takes into account its embeddedness within psychological, political, social, and cultural structures.

Immediately after the Second World War, literary criticism theorized the incomprehensible nature of the Nazi genocide. It was argued that silence was the only appropriate response, the only manner by which one could pay respect to the dead. In *Language and Silence*, George Steiner speaks of the "failure of the word in the face of the inhuman"[208] referring to the collapse of referential coherence and to the breakdown of the mimetic function of language after the Holocaust. Steiner describes how contemporary art is confronted with the impossible task of representing an incomprehensible violence, and situates the Holocaust in a non-linguistic realm: "The world of Auschwitz lies outside speech as it lies outside reason".[209]

The unspeakability of the Holocaust is due to the inadequacy of language, which lacks the means for representing such a traumatic experience. Primo Levi underlines how the meaning of words was different in the camps:

> Just as our hunger is not that feeling of missing a meal, so our way of being cold has need of a new word. We say 'hunger', we say 'tiredness', 'fear', 'pain', we say 'winter' and they are different things. They are free words, created and used by free men who lived in comfort and suffering in their homes. If the Lagers had lasted longer, a new, harsh language would have been born; and only this language could express what it means to toil the whole day in the wind, with the temperature below freezing, wearing only a shirt, underpants, cloth jacket and trousers, and in one's body nothing but weakness, hunger and the knowledge of the end drawing nearer.[210]

---

[206] R. Chambers, "Orphaned Memories, Foster-Writing, Phantom Pain", in N. Miller, and J. Tougaw, eds. *Extremities: Trauma, Testimony and Community*, Urbana: University of Illinois Press, 2002, p. 103.
[207] *Ibid.*
[208] G. Steiner, *Language and Silence: Essays on Language, Literature, and the Inhuman*, New Haven, London: Yale University Press, 1998, p. 51.
[209] *Ibid.*, p. 123.
[210] P. Levi, *Survival in Auschwitz*, p. 123.

The experience of the Holocaust is so traumatic as to defy and overwhelm language: in the attempt to come to terms with trauma, language breaks down. Therefore, conventional techniques are inadequate with respect to such extreme experiences: in order to understand the post-Holocaust world, a new language is necessary. In Holocaust fiction, it is the way in which language and narrative break down that conveys the very meaning and "truth" of trauma. Postmodern literary representations of the Holocaust such as Martin Amis's *Time's Arrow* can thus recognize and embody the linguistic, literary and ethical problems inherent in representing trauma.

According to Geoffrey Hartman, trauma "comes through the radical inadequacy of what is heard or read, when the words searched for cannot address or redress other shocks"[211]. "Literature", says Hartman, "both recognizes and offsets that inadequacy"[212]: if language fails, resulting in silence, then no working-through is possible. Literature is the site where trauma can be made perceivable, and silence audible, through the capacity of readers

> to read for what is without words, or as yet beyond their reach: for the wound as well as the power of signification that contains or composes it. Such reading presupposes of *literary* words that in some way they bear the wound or are scarred by it. [213]

In the context of Holocaust fiction, linguistic experiments are necessary: since trauma affects the abilities and functions of language, a non-mimetic form of representation is the only possible one. Martin Amis's experimental novel *Time's Arrow* constitutes a powerful example of how postmodern fiction can deal with traumatic memory by negotiating the ethical demands of addressing the Holocaust with the aesthetic features of a postmodern text.

Amis's style serves a purpose above and beyond its apparent postmodern experimentation: by shifting from linguistic to epistemological experiments, from playing with readers on the level of language to engaging them on the level of meaning, Amis unsettles his readers and forces them to confront the Holocaust anew. *Time's Arrow* thus embodies the crisis of language and representation (and thus also the crisis of history and literature) in the post-Holocaust world, where a regeneration of language is required.

During the Nazi regime, language was deliberately corrupted in order to be used as a political tool. Words were crushed and misused, their meaning distorted: if nowadays language has become suspect, it is also because words have been used to betray and deceive. The Nazis distorted language to such a

---

[211] G. Hartman, "Trauma Within the Limits of Literature", p. 259.
[212] *Ibid.*
[213] *Ibid.*, pp. 259-60.

degree that it could no longer be considered as a means for connecting individuals to experience.

The corruption of language was one of the most effective methods the Nazis employed in the dehumanization process: "[o]f all the weapons in the Nazi arsenal, the most deadly by far was the spoken word"[214]. Through the estrangement from language, the victims' humanity was dismantled, because human experience is neither intelligible nor "experienceable" outside of language.

The vocabulary of concentration camps was totally peculiar. Auschwitz survivor Elie Wiesel refers to it as "the language of night":

> The language of night was not human; it was primitive, almost animal – hoarse shouting, screaming, muffled moaning, savage howling, the sounds of beating [...] Such was the language of the concentration camp. It negated all other language and took its place. Rather than link people, it became a wall between them.[215]

According to Wiesel, although the linguistic barrier between the survivors and the rest of the world is insurmountable, it is the responsibility of the survivor to try to scale it and find a way to communicate the horror of the Holocaust.

In *A Double Dying*, Alvin Rosenfeld argues that the Nazi language "clos[ed] the space [...] between violent words and violent deeds"[216]. The Nazis literalized metaphors: Rosenfeld proposes the metaphorical expression "pouring salt into open wounds" as an example of a phrase that under Nazism lost its metaphorical meaning to collapse with its real denotation, and wonders how this expression can continue to function as a metaphor, when the actions described have been actually enacted[217]: "[h]ow, after all, can we accept a realism more extreme than any surrealism ever invented?"[218].

By disguising morally reprehensible acts in vague and ambiguous terms, the Nazis also imposed a linguistic cover upon atrocity[219]. The counterfeit innocence of the Nazis' language aimed at concealing and interpreting their actions, at hiding the true meaning of their acts, in order to prevent perpetrators from equating what they were doing with their knowledge of murder and evil. Through bureaucratic manipulation of language, the Nazis developed a vocabulary of "euphemisms" to deflect the imagination from their murderous

---

[214] S. Horowitz, *Voicing the Void*, p. 157.
[215] E. Wiesel, "Why I Write", in E. Wiesel, *From the Kingdom of Memory: Reminescences*, New York: Summit Books, 1990, p. 15.
[216] A. Rosenfeld, *A Double Dying: Reflections on Holocaust Literature*, Bloomington: Indiana University Press, 1980, p. 135.
[217] *Ibid.*, p. 135.
[218] *Ibid.*, p. 24.
[219] S. Horowitz, *Voicing the Void.*, p. 157.

purposes: by renaming, they sought to make verbally manageable what was in reality atrocious[220]. Moreover, the Nazis recognized "the urgency of deluding the victims about their fate in order to achieve smoother implementation of their plans"[221]. So, Jews were singled out for "special handling", they were "resettled", and then "liquidated": they were never merely *murdered*.

An interesting analysis of the altered state of the German language during Nazism is Victor Klemperer's study *The Language of the Third Reich*[222], where the philologist observes how Nazism contaminated even the most basic language with an excessive use of abbreviations, euphemisms, and metaphors. Thereby, the Nazis created a language that forced all its users, even the victims, to write and think in specific ways: according to Klemperer, the language of the Third Reich helped to create its culture.

At the very beginning of Martin Amis's novel *Time's Arrow*, the narrator prides himself on the precision with which he uses language: "I have a superb vocabulary (monad, retractile, necropolis, palindrome, antidisestablishmentarianism) and a nonchalant command of all grammatical rules" (16). The focus on the narrator's vocabulary draws our attention to the role of language: this will acquire significance later on, when we become aware of Tod's involvement in the Nazi genocide. Pairing this discovery with our own previous knowledge of the importance of language for the Nazi enterprise, we are able to interpret the narrator's "revealing examples of camp argot":

> The main Ovenroom is called *Heavenblock*, its main approach road *Heavenstreet*. Chamber and Sprinkleroom are known [...] as *the central hospital*. *Sommerfrische* is our name for a tour of duty here, in any season: summer air, suggesting a perennial vacation from an inadequate reality. (133)

Since the time's reversal causes a reversal of all logic, the Nazi terminology makes plain sense for the narrator, who does not understand the real meaning of what is actually going on: it is the reader who has the responsibility to read between the lines and disclose the linguistic duplicities of Nazism that the narrator cannot correctly interpret. By exposing the "Nazification" of language, Amis's novel reveals precisely how language has been corrupted, and maybe permanently damaged, during the Nazi era.

---

[220] P. Joffe, "Language Damage: Nazis and Naming in Martin Amis's *Time's Arrow*", *Nomina Africana* 9.2 (1995), p. 3.
[221] *Ibid.*
[222] V. Klemperer, *The Language of the Third Reich: LTI – Lingua Tertii Imperii: A Philologist's Notebook*, trans. M. Brady, London: Athlone Press, 2000.

2.2 Martin Amis

Martin Amis was born in Oxford on August 25, 1949, the son of the writer Kingsley Amis. He was educated in England, Spain and the USA, and graduated from Exeter College, Oxford, in 1971. Since 1973, the publication date of his first novel, *The Rachel Papers*, he represents one of the most successful voices of contemporary British fiction. Many of the features that characterize Amis's subsequent fiction are already discernible in his first novel. With *The Rachel Papers*, Amis established himself as a comic writer whose subject is not the traditional subject of comedy. Through the words of the novel's first-person narrator Charles Highway, Amis observes: "Surely, nice things are dull, and nasty things are funny. The nastier a thing is, the funnier it gets"[223].

The Rachel Papers was followed by *Dead Babies* in 1975. Amis's third novel, *Success*, was published in 1978, followed by *Other People: A Mystery Story* in 1981. The collection of short stories *Einstein's Monsters* was published in 1987. From 1984 to 1995, Amis wrote three novels set in London: *Money: A Suicide Note* (1984), *London Fields* (1989), and *The Information* (1995).

The novel I analyze in this book, *Time's Arrow, or The Nature of the Offence*, was published in 1991 and short-listed for the Booker Prize for Fiction. It narrates the life story of a Nazi doctor in reverse time, from the point of view of the doctor's "dissociated self", and it possibly represents the best literary realization of Amis's claim that "[w]hat you're always looking for, is a way to see the world differently"[224]. As we will see, *Time's Arrow* raised fierce debates about the appropriateness of dealing with the theme of the Holocaust in such a peculiar way. In the following chapters, I will try to show that *Time's Arrow* is not an immoral novel, and that its style is appropriate to the content: as Amis put it, "style *is* morality"[225].

More recent works of fiction by Amis include *Night Train* (1997), *Heavy Waters and Other Stories* (1998), *Yellow Dog* (2003), *House of Meetings* (2006) and *The Pregnant Widow*, which should be published in 2008. The moving autobiography *Experience* (2000) is mainly about Martin Amis's relationship with his famous father Kingsley and tells of their difficult family life. Faithful to the postmodern style he adopts in fiction writing, Amis rejects the traditional chronological structure of memoir and organizes the events of his life thematically, so that his autobiography reads almost like a novel.

Amis is also a literary critic. He published three collections of essays: *The Moronic Inferno and Other Visits to America* (1986), *Visiting Mrs Nabokov and*

---

[223] M. Amis, *The Rachel Papers*, New York: Knopf, 1974, p. 91.
[224] M. Amis, qtd. in J. Diedrick, *Understanding Martin Amis*, Columbia: University of South Carolina Press, 2004, p. 257, n.1.
[225] M. Amis, *Experience: A Memoir*, New York: Miramax, 2000, p. 122.

Other Excursions (1993), and *The War Against Cliché* (2001). *Koba the Dread: Laughter and the Twenty Million*, published in 2002, is a political essay about communism in the twentieth century. The layering of selves and time in Amis's novels parallels his double role of "writer-creator and critic-reader", his "persistent double perspective": "[h]e writes and he analyses. He feels and he thinks. He creates and he criticises. [...] His work will make you think. It may also make you cry"[226].

Amis's novels are written in a self-conscious experimental style which blurs the boundaries between content and form and resists classification. Mixing humor with horror, Amis challenges existing critical paradigms and institutionalized concepts such as satire, irony and parody. *Time's Arrow* is a clear example of the breakdown of boundaries and of the collapse of genres typical of Amis's novels, as it mixes black comedy with tragedy.

Criticism about Martin Amis is characterized by ambivalent feelings. For many critics, he is one of the most influential and innovative voices in contemporary British fiction. His detractors, however, consider his emphasis on language and style as shallow and even immoral, particularly in the case of *Time's Arrow*. The controversies surrounding Amis prove that his fiction challenges not only the art and criticism of the past, but also that of the present. Amis transgresses the conventions of realism, modernism, and even those of postmodernism: his novels are written according to *his own* understanding of postmodernism.

2.3 *Time's Arrow*: an introduction

Time's Arrow traces the life of a Nazi Doctor in reverse time, from his death to his birth, thus reversing the arrow of time. Its topic (the Holocaust) and the strategy of the time's reversal are not the only characteristics that allow us to consider this novel a trauma narrative: the intertextual relations, particularly with Robert Jay Lifton's *The Nazi Doctors*[227], the ironic and humorous treatment of a tragic subject, the peculiar status of the narrator, the important role of the reader and the use of style for conveying meaning represent other challenging structural and formal elements that characterize *Time's Arrow* as trauma fiction.

First of all, I will briefly outline the plot of the novel, which has been defined as a "*Bildungsroman* in reverse"[228]. *Time's Arrow* opens in America, at Tod

---

[226] M. Reynolds, *Martin Amis: The Essential Guide,* London: Vintage, 2003, pp. 6-7.
[227] R. J. Lifton, *The Nazi Doctors: Medical Killing and the Psychology of Genocide*, New York: Basic Books, 2000.
[228] J. Marta, "Postmodernizing the Literature-and-Medicine Canon: Self-Conscious Narration, Unruly Texts, and the *Viae Ruptae* of Narrative Medicine", *Literature and Medicine* 16.1 (1997), p. 64.

Friendly's deathbed, from where he is taken to the hospital and then released. Soon afterwards, he has a heart attack. Day by day, Tod rejuvenates: he feels increasingly younger and healthier, and his body grows stronger. After retirement, Tod accedes to a medical career in New Jersey. Then comes a car crash, followed by "the first instalment" (28) of his love life: a fight with a woman named Irene, who tells him that she knows his secret, because he says it in his sleep, and that she knows he changed his name and is on the run. Irene visits him more and more frequently, until she suddenly disappears after a night at the movies. Every December Tod gets a letter informing him that the weather continues to be "temperate" in New York, to where he moves soon afterwards. In New York, he changes his name into John Young and works as a surgeon. Throughout this time, he has a series of affairs with a number of women.

In the summer of 1948 John set sails "for Europe, and for war" (107). In Lisbon, he becomes Hamilton de Souza, a rich merchant living in a luxurious villa with three maids and a gardener. After a few years, de Souza leaves Portugal for Italy. He goes to Salerno and then to the Vatican, where he gives his Portuguese visa to Father Duryea, an Irish priest, and receives from him his new documents, before leaving for Germany, and for war. As Odilo Unverdorben, he travels to Bologna by train, and then by truck to Rovereto. From there, he has to move "from village to village, farm to farm, on foot, by cart, in preposterous automobiles" (121-2). On the Brenner, he hides in farmhouses until at last he arrives "at Auschwitz Central somewhat precipitately and by motorbike [...] shortly after the Bolsheviks had entrained their ignoble withdrawal" (124).

At Auschwitz, the world starts making sense to the narrator, for whom chronology and logic are reversed. In the death camp, Odilo resumes his medical career and assists "Uncle Pepi" conducting researches and curing patients: seen backwards, the genocide does not seem destruction, but creation, and the terrible experiments on prisoners appear as methods for healing them. The Nazi dream, the narrator tells us, is "[t]o make a people from the weather. From thunder and from lightning. With gas, with electricity, with shit, with fire" (128). However, in the spring of 1944, when his wife Herta pays her first visit to Auschwitz, she disapproves of the work he is doing there. During Odilo's time at Auschwitz, their daughter Eva dies.

In 1942, at age twenty-five, he leaves Auschwitz and journeys to Berlin by train. There, he meets Herta again and finds her completely transformed: she is pregnant. Odilo and Herta move through various stages of marriage, courtship, and acquaintance. Meanwhile, the Jews are "deconcentrated", and "channelled back into society", and Odilo helps "dismantle and disperse the ghettos" (149). As he journeys homeward to the Reich, he pays "a brief courtesy call" to Treblinka. After a short time spent at home with Herta, during which "the act of love" happens only once because of his impotence, Odilo goes to Schloss

Hartheim, where, according to the reversed logic of the narrator, the physically and mentally impaired are created from ashes. "Was the Chamber faulty?" wonders the narrator: "the people we produced just weren't any good any more" (154).

After Schloss Hartheim, "the world has stopped making sense again" (157). Odilo joins the Reserve Medical Corps, and then attends medical school. The narrator records the gradual improvements in the life conditions of Jews: they are allowed to keep pets, to buy meat, cheese and eggs, and to have friendly relations with Aryans. Odilo now sees Herta every day at school, but after a while she stops talking to him: when he sees her, "she moves right through [his] gaze" (165), until she finally vanishes.

In 1929, at age thirteen, Odilo goes on a camping trip along the Sola, near Auschwitz and Birkenau: the narrator interprets it as "a sentimental journey" (169), and observes how "all the power and wonder had been washed away by time and weather" (170). Finally, we see Odilo as a little child, living in Solingen with Father and Mother. He becomes more and more intimate with Mother. At last, Odilo will enter her, and his father "will come in and kill [him] with his body" (172).

In order to clarify what really happens in the novel, Neil Easterbrook reverses the time's arrow once again and summarizes the story of Odilo's life in its "proper" chronological order[229]. Following Easterbrook's article, I will try to outline the *fabula* of Amis's novel, organizing the events in their "real" sequence. Thereby, it will be clarified how Odilo's life is similar to that of an "average" Nazi doctor as described by Robert J. Lifton in his study on medical killing and the psychology of genocide, *The Nazi Doctors*.

Odilo Unverdorben was born in 1916 in Solingen, the birthplace of Adolf Eichmann, the Gestapo overseer directly responsible for deporting and murdering hundreds of Jews. Odilo's father dies soon, leaving him to be raised by his mother, a nurse, who inspires Odilo's interest in medicine. On a camping trip when he is thirteen, Odilo visits the site that will later become Auschwitz. The only other remarkable events of his youth concern rejection by women and abuse by bigger boys: "Odilo is, it turns out, innocent, emotional, popular, and stupid" (157). Despite his stupidity, he enters medical school, and marries Herta, a young secretary. Once married, he finds himself impotent and subjects his wife to a series of beatings and humiliations. They will eventually have a child, Eva, who will die soon.

---

[229] N. Easterbrook, "'I know that it is to do with trash and shit, and that it is wrong in time': Narrative Reversal in Martin Amis's *Time's Arrow*", *Conference of College Teachers of English (CCTE) Studies* 55 (1995), pp. 53-4.

After graduation, Odilo goes to work at Schloss Hartheim, the medical laboratory where Nazi doctors experimented with the techniques later applied in the death camps. Commissioned as an officer, he then serves in the Waffen SS. In 1942, he joins the KZ and becomes assistant to "Uncle Pepi" at Auschwitz. By 1944 he is helping kill "the Hungarian Jews, and at an incredible rate, something like 10,000 a day" (137). The slaughter accelerates until, just before Russian troops arrive, Odilo escapes, making his way to Rome, where in exchange for some gold an Irish emissary of the Vatican helps him obtain a new identity.

Taking the first of his pseudonyms, in 1946 Odilo is in Portugal under the name of Hamilton de Souza, comfortably ensconced within a villa. In 1948, he sails for America as John Young. Aided by Reverend Kreditor, Young finds work in a New York hospital. At some point in the 1960s, Kreditor discovers that accusations have been made against Young, who then becomes Tod Friendly and flees New York, ending up in a suburb in New Jersey. In his 70s, he dies of a heart attack.

As I have already anticipated, Odilo's life resembles very much that of many Nazi doctors, and these similarities are more evident if his story is seen "forwards": he joins the Nazi party, practices medical killing in the concentration camps, and escapes to the United States, where, using assumed identities, he practices medicine again and dies at an advanced age. In *The Nazi Doctors*, which is Amis's main intertext, Robert J. Lifton notes how, after the war, most Nazi doctors, even those who had been directly involved in murder, continued to see themselves as decent physicians, and could resume medical practice: "Hence, the strange three-part odyssey from pre-Nazi physician-healer, to Nazi physician-killer, to post-Nazi physician-healer"[230].

As we will see, Amis draws consistently on Lifton's descriptions of the Nazi doctors to create his fictionalized version of a Nazi doctor's life, and he recognizes his "great debt" to Lifton in the "Afterword" to the novel, where he acknowledges Lifton's study as his main source: "[my] novel would not and could not have been written without it" (175).

2.4 Intertextuality: Robert Jay Lifton's *The Nazi Doctors*

At the center of Lifton's inquiry is the question of how Nazi doctors could be transformed from healers into killers, while maintaining their professional identity. Before Auschwitz, most of the Nazi doctors had been ordinary practitioners. Lifton underlines the ordinariness of most Nazi doctors by stating: "Neither brilliant nor stupid, neither inherently evil nor particularly ethically sensitive, they were by no means the demonic figures – sadistic, fanatic, lusting

---

[230] R. J. Lifton, *The Nazi Doctors*, p. 457.

to kill – people have often thought them to be"[231]. In this perspective, Lifton refers to Hannah Arendt's idea of the "banality of evil"[232] and claims that although Nazi doctors were indeed banal people, what they did was not banal at all: once accepted their active role as perpetrators of the Nazi genocide, they separated themselves from other human beings[233]. In his study, Lifton analyzes how and why such unexceptional men could become part of the most extreme killing project.

"The unfortunate truth", observes Lifton, "is that people can all too readily be socialized to killing", because of the "human genius for adaptation"[234]. The emergence of the concept of "socialization to genocide"[235] makes genocide a serious problem for all contemporary societies, because it reveals that mass killing is a more easily doable project than previously imagined: we cannot assume that Nazi evil has no relationship to us. In fact, the Holocaust demonstrates how very ordinary people, who are not ideological fanatics, can be effectively absorbed into the structures and the dynamics of mass killing. According to Lifton, this awareness does not diminish individual responsibility for one's action: the fact that the Nazi doctors were unremarkable men does not mean that they are not responsible for what they did.

Lifton does not agree with those who argue that understanding means forgiving, and that the Holocaust should merely be isolated and condemned, because studying it may replace condemnation with insights[236]. For Lifton, understanding should include moral reckoning, so that forgiving would not follow. Studying the source of evil in an ethically engaged way is thus a means to combat evil, and it could help us to prevent other genocides and to create better societies.

Physicians had a central role in facilitating genocide; they were crucial to atrocity. The Nazi doctors epitomized the principle of *"killing as a therapeutic imperative"*[237]: Jews were considered as diseases that had to be removed in order to heal the Aryan race. In the Nazi medical vision, the extermination of the Jews was seen as purification. By adapting to this crazy logic, doctors fell into what Lifton calls the *"healing-killing paradox"*[238]: if Jews were diseased organs to be amputated for the well-being of the body, killing them was the prerequisite for healing the German society, for saving the body politic. In this light, murder

---

[231] R. J. Lifton, *The Nazi Doctors*, pp. 4-5.
[232] See H. Arendt, *Eichmann in Jerusalem: A Report on the Banality of Evil*, New York: Viking, 1963.
[233] R. J. Lifton, *The Nazi Doctors.*, p. 12.
[234] *Ibid.*, p. x.
[235] *Ibid.*
[236] *Ibid.*, p. xi.
[237] *Ibid.*, p. 15.
[238] *Ibid.*, pp. 150, 430-3.

appeared life-affirming, and the genocide assumed a sense of necessity and appropriateness.

Most Nazi doctors underwent a psychological shift from revulsion to acceptance: this shift involved a *socialization* to Auschwitz[239]. Language and ideology played a fundamental role in this process: the Nazis based their justification for direct medical killing on the concept of "life unworthy of life" (*lebensuwertes Leben*)[240], and referred to the murder of physically or mentally impaired people as "mercy killing" (*Gnadentod*)[241], while "special treatment" (*Sonderbehandlung*)[242] was the word for the killing of people, especially Jews, in the death camps.

By detoxifying killing and infusing it with a quasi-mystical aura, the Nazis' "numbed" language favoured the routinization of murder by "rendering murder nonmurderous"[243]. The very term "Final Solution" (*Endlösung*) had psychological purposes: it stood for mass murder without sounding like it, and it put the focus on problem solving, so that doctors could come to accept the mass murder as a solution to the "Jewish problem"[244]. For Nazi doctors, killing was a difficult but necessary and even heroic form of "personal ordeal": "a true SS officer [...] takes on, when necessary for his Führer and his race, precisely those tasks he finds repellent"[245].

Much of the language and procedure of the death camps can be interpreted as easing the reality of murder by denying actual atrocity, in order to distance the doctors from their own deeds. Having accepted that Jews were the world's fundamental evil, physicians were susceptible to persuasion that killing Jews would heal the Aryan race, and could thus direct the genocide and at the same time maintain their identity as doctors: they saw themselves not as murderers, but as purifiers of society.

The Nazi doctors called forth "every possible mechanism to *avoid taking in psychologically what they were doing* – every form of psychic numbing and derealization"[246]. Their socialization to an environment of mass killing was enhanced also by the camp's isolation from the outside world: Auschwitz was perceived as a realm of experience so extreme that it was literally a separate reality. Moreover, psychic numbing was favoured by a sense that one did not come first in the hierarchy of horrors.

---

[239] *Ibid.*, p. 195.
[240] *Ibid.*, p. 21.
[241] *Ibid.*, p. 50.
[242] *Ibid.*, p. 150.
[243] *Ibid.*, p. 445.
[244] *Ibid.*, p. 206.
[245] *Ibid.*, p. 437.
[246] *Ibid.*, p. 200.

According to Lifton, the key to understanding how Nazi doctors became mass murderers is the psychological process of *doubling*: "Auschwitz as an *institution* – as an atrocity-producing situation – ran on doubling"[247]. Through doubling, the self separates "into two functioning wholes, so that the part-self acts as an entire self"[248]. Nazi doctors needed both selves in order to function psychologically: the "Auschwitz self" was necessary in order to perpetrate the killings, while the "prior self" allowed them to continue to see themselves as human beings and doctors.

Lifton defines doubling as "the mechanism by which a doctor, in his actions, moved from the ordinary to the demonic"[249]: it was the psychological means that allowed physicians to "embrace evil with an extreme lack of restraint"[250]. Doubling was "the psychological vehicle for the Nazi doctor's Faustian bargain with the diabolical environment in exchange for his contribution to the killing"[251]. The fact that doubling took place mainly outside of consciousness does not abrogate the Nazi doctors' responsibility: "One is always ethically responsible for Faustian bargains"[252]. Since doubling is an *active* process, by deciding to double "Nazi doctors made a Faustian choice for evil"[253].

To the Nazi "ethos", the claim to logic, rationality and science was extremely important, but Nazi rationality was based on a deadly logic: "from insane premises to monstrous conclusions Hitler was relentlessly logical"[254]. Amis's ironic portrayal of the doubled psyche of a Nazi doctor aims precisely at revealing how Nazi thought was actually a grotesque parody of reason.

According to Lifton, we are "meaning-hungry creatures"[255]: our mind constantly tries to make sense of events, to organize them into meaningful patterns, and to find rational reasons for everything we do. The grotesque transformations of reason and moral values produced by Nazi ideology allowed the Nazi doctors to participate in the mass murder of millions of human beings without feeling guilty: this testifies to the adaptive capacities of the human mind. "Auschwitz makes all too clear the principle that the human psyche can create meaning out of anything"[256]: although extremely irrational things happened there, nothing seemed strange to Nazis.

---

[247] *Ibid.*, p. 425.
[248] *Ibid.*, p. 418.
[249] *Ibid.*, p. 427.
[250] *Ibid.*, p. 420.
[251] *Ibid.*, p. 418
[252] *Ibid.*
[253] *Ibid.*, p. 424.
[254] J. H. McRandle, *The Track of the Wolf: Essays on National Socialism and Its Leader, Adolf Hitler*, Evanston: Northwestern University Press, 1965, p. 125. Qtd. in R. J. Lifton, *The Nazi Doctors*, p. 439.
[255] R. J. Lifton, *The Nazi Doctors*, p. 459.
[256] *Ibid.*

Lifton notes how the healing-killing paradox made sense for the Nazi doctor's Auschwitz self: "[t]o the extent that one embraces the far reaches of the Nazi vision of killing Jews in order to heal the Nordic race, the paradox disappears"[257]. In the morally and logically reversed world of the death camps, even the name *anus mundi* that was given to Auschwitz was associated with a positive mission[258]. Similarly, the narrator of *Time's Arrow* expresses a positive view of Auschwitz as the anus of the world: "we sometimes refer to Auschwitz as Anus Mundi. And I can think of no finer tribute than that" (133).

Lifton's study not only provides a new insight into the motivations and actions of Nazi doctors, but also raises broader questions about human behaviour: "[n]o individual self is inherently evil, murderous, genocidal. Yet under certain conditions virtually any self is capable of becoming all of these"[259]. In fact, "most of what Nazi doctors did would be within the potential capability [...] of most doctors and of most people"[260]: if Nazi doctors doubled in murderous ways, others could do so as well. Although this awareness troubles us, it is important to acknowledge that we are all fallible human beings and to recognize our own potential for evil. In his novel, Amis clarifies this idea by forcing readers to come to terms with their own involvement in evil: *Time's Arrow* represents a warning against indifference and a call for moral thinking.

However, it is also important to distinguish between potential and actual evil, and to underline that individuals have a moral responsibility if they choose evil: "[w]e are *not* all Nazis. That accusation eliminates precisely the kind of moral distinctions we need to make"[261]. In fact, the self can always reject doubling and move toward principles of integrity, unity and awareness of oneself and others as human beings[262]. If understanding the psychology of Nazi Holocaust perpetrators can help us avoid the next Holocaust, Amis's novel may represent a step forward in this direction.

Time's Arrow and *The Nazi Doctors*

As Amis claims in the novel's "Afterword", *Time's Arrow* "would not and could not have been written" (175) without Robert J. Lifton's *The Nazi Doctors*. The description of Odilo Unverdorben in Amis's novel closely resembles the psychological profile of Nazi doctors offered by Lifton in his study. Unverdorben may well be defined as the archetypal Nazi doctor: he has done everything a Nazi doctor could do, from pre-war "euthanasia" at Schloss Hartheim to the horrific experiments and medicalized killings at Auschwitz.

---

[257] *Ibid.*, p. 430.
[258] *Ibid.*, p. 431.
[259] *Ibid.*, p. 497.
[260] *Ibid.*, p. 427.
[261] *Ibid.*, p. 503.
[262] *Ibid.*, p. 499.

The first scene of the novel introduces the theme of the power and omnipresence of doctors. As Tod Friendly comes back to life in the hospital, he perceives the dreadful power of doctors standing around his bed:

> I moved forward, out of the blackest sleep, to find myself surrounded by *doctors*... American doctors: I sensed their vigour, scarcely held in check, like the profusion of their body hair; and the forbidding touch of their forbidding hands [...]. The doctors seemed to be availing themselves of my immobility. [...] How I hate doctors. Any doctors. All doctors. (11)

The scene of Tod's awakening is also conflated with images of Nazi doctors:

> Presiding over the darkness out of which I had loomed there was a figure, a male shape, with an entirely unmanageable aura, containing such things as beauty, terror, love, filth, and above all power. This male shape or essence seemed to be wearing a white coat (a medic's stark white smock). And black boots. (12)

This "figure" emerges from Tod's memory of his past, and Amis has clearly taken it from Lifton's description of the transportation of the mentally and physically disabled to killing centers:

> SS personnel manned the buses, frequently wearing white uniforms or white coats in order to appear to be doctors, nurses, or medical attendants. There were reports of "men with white coats and SS boots".[263]

The backwards narration and the status of the narrator are the most important formal devices used by Amis to convey the idea that only a split subjectivity ("doubling") and a complete reversal of moral values (the "healing-killing paradox") could allow doctors to take part in the murderous ideology of the camps, keep their mental sanity, and go back to ordinary medical practice after the war. I will analyze the time's reversal strategy and the status of the narrator in chapter eight. In the next paragraphs, I will focus on the intertextual references to Lifton's study in Amis's depiction of a Nazi doctor.

Tod's ability to detach from the lives of other human beings – as the narrator puts it, "the body I live and move in, Tod's body, feels nothing" (26) – mirrors Lifton's theory about the Nazi doctors' psychic numbing and mechanisms of "derealization", owing to which Nazi doctors performed the selections, killings, and experiments with a complete lack of feeling[264].

---

[263] R. J. Lifton, *The Nazi Doctors*, p. 70.
[264] *Ibid.*, p. 442.

According to Lifton, not a single one of the Nazi doctors he interviewed has ever arrived at a clear ethical evaluation of his deeds: the events were narrated "almost in the manner of a third person. The narrator, morally speaking, was not quite present"[265]. The status of the narrator in Amis's novel reflects precisely this situation: the narrator makes no overt ethical comments, because he has no moral values according to which he can evaluate what he is doing.

The status of the narrator in Amis's novel also gives symbolic existence to another characteristic of the Nazi doctors' psychological profile outlined by Lifton: the separation between Tod and the narrator reflects Lifton's description of the Nazi doctors' psychological doubling. Lifton's theory about doubling can thus help us shed light on the status of the narrator in *Time's Arrow*.

According to Lifton, "[t]he Auschwitz self had to be both autonomous and connected to the prior self that gave rise to it"[266]. Amis follows this theory in creating a narrator who is inside Tod's head, and thus connected to him, but at the same time autonomous: "I have no access to his thoughts—but I am awash with his emotions" (15). Moreover, Lifton argues that the healing-killing paradox was "crucial in setting the tone for doubling"[267]: the moral reversal of healing and killing was so closely linked to the internal splitting of the subject that one was impossible without the other. The healing-killing reversal was only possible if doctors underwent doubling, but at the same time it was the ability to double that led to moral reversal.

In the novel, the healing-killing reversal is symbolized by the strategy of the time's reversal, a formal device which causes morality to be turned upside-down. The ironic title of the third chapter of *Time's Arrow*, "Because I am a healer, everything I do heals", represents the healing-killing reversal as perceived by the doctors' themselves: they felt that their killings were legitimated by their medical identity. Hence, Amis follows Lifton in witnessing the fact that "doctors killed and did so in the name of healing"[268].

The transformation of medicine into a destructive practice happens automatically when time, and thus logic, is reversed: seen backwards, medicine is "a war against health" (103) and the hospital is "an atrocity-producing situation" (102), which is precisely Lifton's definition for Auschwitz[269]. On the contrary, in *Time's Arrow* it is only at Auschwitz that medicine seems to be the right way round: it heals and saves. Amis's satirical point is, of course, that now everything is wrong. Nothing should look right in the camps: only in a topsy-turvy world like that of Amis's novel can the horrific "medical" practices of Auschwitz appear as morally right.

---

[265] *Ibid.*, p. 8.
[266] *Ibid.*, p. 419.
[267] *Ibid.*, p. 430.
[268] *Ibid.*, p. 503.
[269] *Ibid.*, p. 425.

Amis also reproduces almost verbatim some details and phrases from Lifton's *The Nazi Doctors*. For example, the narrator of *Time's Arrow* observes: "*Some of the patients were doctors.* [...] Those patient doctors are getting quite out of hand. For some reason they are especially zealous in their interference with the children" (143-4). This echoes Lifton's analysis of the prisoner doctors, who could be in a privileged position as long as they submitted to the camps' ideology and practice[270].

The medical experiments to which Odilo contributes at Auschwitz are taken from Lifton's study as well. In particular, Amis has put in his text revealing traces of Josef Mengele's interest in twins and of his experiments on prisoners, such as injecting methylene blue into browned-eyed children's eyes in order to change their eye color and sterilizing young men and women:

> We measure twins together, 'Uncle Pepi' and I, for hours and hours: measure, measure, measure. [...] As to the so-called 'experimental' operations of 'Uncle Pepi': he had a success rate that approached – and quite possibly attained – 100 per cent. A shockingly inflamed eyeball at once rectified by a single injection. Innumerable ovaries and testes seamlessly grafted into place. (142-3)

Similarly, Lifton mentions Mengele's experiments on eye color in order to change it "in an Aryan direction": "Mengele actually injected methylene blue into their eyes, causing severe pain and inflammation"[271]. Lifton adds that Mengele had also carried out sterilization experiments on both men and women.

Amis's description of Uncle Pepi's lab is also taken from Lifton's report of a prisoner doctor's description of his dissection room. Here are Amis's and Lifton's paragraphs: "Uncle Pepi has surpassed himself with his new laboratory: the marble table, the nickel taps, the blood-stained porcelain sinks" (142). For Dr. Miklos Nyiszli, his main prisoner pathologist, Mengele prepared a special dissection room, including a "dissecting table of polished marble", a basin with "nickel taps" and "three porcelain sinks"[272].

Amis's allusion to Mengele is made more explicit by the name he gives to the chief doctor with whom Odilo works, "Uncle Pepi". In fact, Lifton remarks that Mengele was called "Uncle Mengele" by the Gypsy children[273]. Furthermore, Lifton mentions that there were rumors about Mengele's sexual impotence[274], and that the Nazi doctors "wavered between the sense of omnipotent control

---

[270] See R. J. Lifton, "Prisoner Doctors: The Agony of Selections", "Prisoner Doctors: Struggles to Heal", and "Prisoner Doctors: Collaboration with Nazi Doctors", in R. J. Lifton, *The Nazi Doctors*, pp. 214-253.
[271] R. J. Lifton, *The Nazi Doctors*, p. 362.
[272] *Ibid.*, p. 350.
[273] *Ibid.*, p. 375.
[274] *Ibid.*, p. 377.

over the lives and deaths of prisoners and the seemingly opposite sense of impotence"[275]. Likewise, the protagonist of *Time's Arrow* feels omnipotent, but he is sexually impotent: "I am omnipotent. Also impotent. I am powerful and powerless" (148). Finally, Lifton's description of "Mengele's 'special kind of smile'"[276] is echoed by Amis's description of the doctors "presiding over" Tod's death smiling "a certain kind of smile" (12).

Amis remodels and rearranges the borrowings from Lifton in a pointedly ironic way. He ironically compares Nazi doctors and normal medical practice in order to highlight the problems of modern technologized medicine and its potential for violence. This represents a fictionalized depiction of Lifton's conclusion that the psychological and cultural forces which allowed Nazi doctors to work in death camps are present within individuals and societies in all times and places. In fact, Amis follows Lifton in arguing that genocide could happen again (and it *has* happened again in Serbia, Rwanda and Cambodia)[277], and that we should do everything we can to avoid future (nuclear) holocausts.

2.5 The Holocaust between modernism and postmodernism

The Holocaust holds a central place in contemporary thought and it has often been considered as the last crime of the modern world and the first of the postmodern, that is, as the crucial event that brought postmodernity into being. It is generally thought to mark a chronological limit and an epistemological boundary between modernism and postmodernism: "The Holocaust threatens a secular as well as a religious gospel, faith in reason and progress as well as Christianity. It challenges the credibility of redemptive thinking"[278].

The traumatic experiences of World War II brought the master narratives of modernism to crisis and left only their debris: a fragmentary language, a disrupted chronology, and a sense of uncertainty. Holocaust fiction is characterized by ruptures, gaps, and silences. In order to approach it in a relevant manner, it is necessary to situate it within the context of postmodern, posttraumatic culture.

In *The Postmodern Condition*, Lyotard defines the postmodern as "an incredulity towards metanarratives"[279]. He believes that the hopes and goals of modernity have been liquidated in the post-Holocaust era: the universalizing

---

[275] *Ibid.*, p. 447.
[276] *Ibid.*, p. 448.
[277] See R. J. Lifton, "Preface to the 2000 Edition", in R. J. Lifton, *The Nazi Doctors*, pp. vii-x.
[278] G. Hartman, *The Longest Shadow*, p. 124.
[279] J. F. Lyotard, *The Postmodern Condition: A Report on Knowledge*, trans. G. Bennington and B. Massumi, Minneapolis: University of Minnesota Press, 1984, p. xxiv.

grand narratives of modernism have been replaced by small stories, which are characterized by disruption and lack of totality.

Habermas is Lyotard's main interlocutor in the debate "modernity versus postmodernity". He claims that the values of modernity should not be dismissed, because they are still preferable to a postmodernity that, according to him, has given up all values[280]. Both Habermas and Lyotard are reacting to the experience of Nazism: traumatized by the memory of the Holocaust, they are driven by the fear of a return of totalitarianism. However, they arrive at completely different explanations as to the relationship between modernity and totalitarianism: while Lyotard views the Holocaust as the paradigm for the failure of modernity and of the ideals and values of Enlightenment, Habermas considers it as an aberration of those ideals and values. Hence, the Holocaust occupies a central position in the debate between modernism and postmodernism.

Lyotard defines Auschwitz as "the crime opening postmodernity"[281] and calls for "a war on totality"[282]. According to him, modernity has destroyed itself[283], because the very values of modernity are dangerous: universalism, order and unity have lead to a totalizing system and to a totalitarian society. Habermas shares Lyotard's goal of preventing totalitarianisms, but he rejects postmodern uncertainty and holds to the ethical and moral imperatives of modernism, arguing that the mystical, anti-modern features of Nazism are responsible for the Holocaust. Therefore, according to Habermas only a strict maintenance of the modern project can prevent such horrors from happening again.

The Holocaust has become the exemplary topic that pervades the debate of modernity versus postmodernity. The question that haunts this debate is whether the Holocaust is a result or an aberration of modernity. The Holocaust was indeed a modern event in its philosophical and pragmatic existence, but Nazi ideology was also pervaded by "mystical" feelings and absolutely irrational drives. As Martin Amis claims in his "Afterword" to *Time's Arrow*, "the offence was unique [...] in its combination of the atavistic and the modern" (176).

The centrality of the Holocaust within contemporary thought suggests that this event has become emblematic of the course of Western history. The question is whether it is appropriate to incorporate an event as extreme as the Holocaust into "ordinary" history: if we consider the Holocaust as a unique event, then we should agree with Habermas and regard it as an aberration of modernist ideals; if, instead, we agree with Lyotard that the Holocaust is not an aberration, but a consequence of modern thought, then modernity itself should

---

[280] See J. Habermas, "Modernity versus Postmodernity", *New German Critique* 22 (1981): 3-14.
[281] J. F. Lyotard, *The Postmodern Explained*, trans. J. Pefanis and M. Thomas, Minneapolis: University of Minnesota Press, 1988, p. 19.
[282] J. F. Lyotard, *The Postmodern Condition*, p. 82.
[283] *Ibid.*, p. 111.

be held accountable for it. In either case, the Holocaust has left an indelible mark on post-War culture, language, literature, history and philosophy, and its fundamental role in shaping postmodern thought is undeniable.

The postmodern, traumatic style of *Time's Arrow* is possibly the most appropriate form of Holocaust representation, because it escapes the grip of totalizing narratives and deconstructs the possibility of a single version of history. It is precisely this multiplicity that worries some Holocaust scholars, who fear that it might open the door to revisionism: by placing perpetrators' stories into relationship with the stories of the victims, we risk losing the sense of what is morally acceptable.

However, writing a historical novel of trauma in a postmodern style – as Martin Amis does with *Time's Arrow* – does not mean writing in a moral vacuum: if our reading of perpetrators' (hi)stories is subjected to ethical values, the existence of multiple narratives will add to our understanding of the genocide and thus help us prevent it from happening again. The aim of *Time's Arrow* is precisely that of awakening readers into self-consciousness about their own potential complicity in evil, and thus unravelling the oppressive structures and the logic of bureaucratic domination and of objectification of human life that made possible the Nazi genocide.

2.6 What is trauma fiction?

In contemporary Western literature, narratives that record the scars on the body and the mind produced by traumatic experiences have become more and more popular. As readers, we have been accustomed to stories of trauma and "we follow, fascinated (though as many profess disgust), the vogue of violent emotion and shocking events"[284]. Finding an adequate form to represent trauma without leading to a general desensitization represents a challenge for both survivors and for writers of the following generations.

Aesthetic qualities play a central role in depicting trauma in fiction, as my analysis of the relevance of style in *Time's Arrow* will make clear. The fact that Amis's novel represents a traumatic event is not in and of itself sufficient to define it as trauma fiction: trauma fiction is rather defined in terms of the narrative's formal structure, and of the capacity of that structure to convey the fragmentation of meaning and identity brought about by traumatic experiences. Recurring stylistic features of trauma fiction include intertextuality, repetition and a fragmented narrative voice[285]. All of them are present in *Time's Arrow*.

---

[284] N. Miller and J. Tougaw, "Introduction: Extremities", in N. Miller and J. Tougaw, eds. *Extremities*, p. 2.
[285] *Ibid.*

Intertexts are used to give a documentary aspect to the novel, so that it will be perceived as more "truthful" and "authentic". Intertextuality suggests the emergence of traces of the past in the present, a surfacing to consciousness of repressed memories: it is an act of memory which signals the haunting power of trauma. Intertextuality evokes Freud's theory of the repetition-compulsion: it shows how a traumatized individual is always trapped between departure and return, between the possibility of alternative futures and the constrictions of an inescapable fate.

Similarly, repetition mimics the symptoms of trauma: it indicates on a formal level the haunting return of the event and the disruption of chronology which characterize a traumatized individual's mind. Finally, a fragmented narrative voice suggests that history can be written and rewritten from different perspectives, and that trauma can only be worked-through if the traumatic experience is narrated to someone who is willing to listen.

The shocking force of trauma can only be conveyed through formal devices, by mimicking the structure of traumatic experiences. In *Time's Arrow*, trauma fiction overlaps with and borrows from postmodern fiction through a self-conscious use of style and a departure from conventional chronological order: the fragmentation and lack of closure of the postmodern novel merge with the characteristics of trauma fiction to indicate the crisis caused by trauma in the individual's psyche and in society.

Amis's novel reveals that our "era of commemoration"[286] is in reality characterized by forgetfulness: memory and forgetting are part of the same process. In particular, the time's reversal produces an insight into trauma temporality: it represents the surfacing of the past in the present, the haunting quality of unresolved past experiences, which possess those who have been traumatized. This situation reproduces the a-chronology of trauma and reveals the "wisdom of forgetting"[287]: the narrator is innocent and does not feel guilty for his crimes, because for him the past is future and thus he has no memory of it. However, *Time's Arrow* also testifies to the importance of remembering: having no memory of the past, the narrator cannot look onto his future.

Novelists can bring readers close to trauma precisely because they are not confined to describing the events in a linear or conventional fashion. As a fiction of trauma, *Time's Arrow* provides an image of the double significance of trauma's belated temporality: for traumatized individuals, "the past is at once completely present, because trauma stops time, and completely distant, because such time is not susceptible to transformation"[288]. Hence, the dilemma of

---

[286] P. Nora, "The Era of Commemoration" in P. Nora, *Realms of memory*, trans. A. Goldhammer, New York: Columbia University Press, 1998, pp. 609-38.
[287] A. Whitehead, *Trauma Fiction*, Edinburgh: Edinburgh University Press, 2004, p. 19.
[288] M. Rothberg, "Between the Extreme and the Everyday", in N. Miller and J. Tougaw, eds., *Extremities*, p. 65.

traumatized individuals, and thus of trauma fiction, lies in this "traumatic dialectic between the eroding passage of time, which threatens the preservation of memory, and the fixing of time"[289].

In *Time's Arrow*, Tod's dreams are a ghostly presence revealing that the effects of war and the traumas of recent history are not over, but are still haunting individuals and Western societies. Amis thus challenges the psychoanalytic notion that the ghosts of the past can be exorcised: through the figurative return of silenced elements of the past, trauma emerges as a haunting memory that possesses individuals and societies.

Analyzing *Time's Arrow* as a trauma novel, it is useful to take into account the fact that literature is always produced and received within a tapestry of linguistic, social and cultural constructs. The role of readers is particularly relevant in trauma fiction, because they must be active agents and assemble the pieces of the fragmented narrative in order to give meaning to the narrative. Martin Amis engages the reader, asking him or her to participate in the narrative and in the protagonist's trauma, and to put forth a high level of interaction and imagination.

Through the aesthetic recreation of the traumatic event, readers can get closer to the event and come to understand trauma: *Time's Arrow* presents the reader with the opportunity to imagine trauma from the inside, to get *inside* the reality of the trauma, not as a spectator but as a participant. This represents a possibility for heightening social awareness: by struggling in order to reconstruct the linear narrative structure of *Time's Arrow*, the reader becomes personally involved in the traumatic event. The relevance of Amis's novel is thus very much related to its reception: it is precisely by inviting readers to think and take action that trauma fiction performs its task.

Traumatic realism

The Holocaust poses unique challenges to realism and to representation in general. According to Michael Rothberg, *traumatic realism* is the means for coming to terms with a traumatic reality in fiction by going "beyond the assumptions of traditional realist accounts of mimesis and reference"[290] in order to bring forth traces of trauma. The concept of traumatic realism opens up a new space for reading narratives of extremity, creating a universe that violates all expectations and thus disorients the reader. As a narrative of trauma, *Time's Arrow* requires an adjustment of our skills as readers: "faced with the literary effects of what Rothberg has called "traumatic realism" [...] we are forced to reexamine the troubling conjuncture of the extreme and the everyday"[291].

---

[289] *Ibid.*, p. 66.
[290] *Ibid.*
[291] N. Miller and J. Tougaw, *Extremities*, p. 7.

A narrative of trauma transforms its readers and forces them to acknowledge their responsibility, thereby inviting them to take action. Hence, Amis's traumatic novel represents a text "whose origin belongs to the past (and those who died in it) but whose effects belong both to the present and the future – to the living readers"[292]: "Traumatic realism is not turned only towards the past [...] By virtue of its performative address to a post-traumatic context, this kind of writing possesses a future orientation"[293].

According to Rothberg, the two main approaches to the representation of the Holocaust have been the "antirealist" and the "realist". Although experimental writers consider realism inadequate to the task of confronting a traumatized world, Rothberg notes how the realist position has all but disappeared in post-Holocaust literature. The recent interest in questions of truth, authenticity, memory and history makes it necessary to rethink realism in the light of the traumatic experiences of the twentieth and twenty-first centuries.

By revealing the implication of extremity in the ordinary, the "traumatic realism" of Amis's novel offers a way out of the dichotomy realism versus antirealism and provides an aesthetic and cognitive solution to the demands of Holocaust representation. *Time's Arrow* thus represents a response to both realist and antirealist tendencies: it entails some form of traumatic realism into a postmodern discourse, while at the same time challenging the narrative form of traditional realism.

The desire for realism and referentiality is one of the defining features of Holocaust Studies: although traditional realism has been challenged by traumatic realism, the impulse to represent a traumatized world with the greatest possible fidelity remains central in many postmodern trauma narratives, which "tend to try to reconceptualize realism rather than to reject it outright"[294]. However, traumatic realism recognizes the discrepancies between language and reality, and moves towards non-representational or non-referential aesthetic practices.

The struggle for understanding and representing trauma pushes the realist project to its limits: in the postmodern context, there is indeed a wish to represent reality, but this desire is counterfeited by the recognition that mimesis is impossible. Traumatic realism is not a set of fixed forms and techniques: it should rather be intended as a non-conventional approach to the representation of reality. In this sense, the non-mimetic approach of *Time's Arrow*, and in particular its chronological reversal, can be considered as the most remarkable characteristics that allow us to consider this novel as trauma fiction.

---

[292] *Ibid.*
[293] M. Rothberg, "Between the Extreme and the Everyday", p. 67.
[294] A. Gąsiorek, *Post-War British Fiction: Realism and After*, London: Edward Arnold, 1995, p. v.

Moreover, the fact that even in a postmodern, definitely non-realist novel such as *Time's Arrow* the author felt the need to acknowledge his documentary sources reveals the persistence of the problem of reference and documentation in postmodern trauma fiction. In particular, Amis mentions Primo Levi's testimonies and Robert J. Lifton's psychological study on the Nazi Doctors: these references supply the novel with those documentary historical and scientific bases that even postmodern fiction seems to require when dealing with the Holocaust.

However, Amis's search for documentation does not consist of a demand for an archive of facts referring to the event and of a need for a coherent story: what he is looking for is a form of documentation that goes beyond narrative coherence. In fact, representing trauma requires a different kind of reference, because the reality that trauma fiction seeks to register is a traumatic reality, where the everyday and the extreme coexist.

Trauma fiction meets its limits not only in the impossibility of direct reference, but also in the problem of the belated temporality of traumatic experiences. Chronological progression has been ruptured by trauma: Rothberg notes how, properly speaking, there is no era after Auschwitz, because "the material conditions that made the Nazi genocide possible live on after the 'Final Solution' has run its course"[295].

Therefore, traumatic realism must take into account the effects of the Holocaust on the time of representation: trauma can only be represented through a traumatized structure that reproduces the disrupted temporality of trauma. It is precisely in this sense that the style of *Time's Arrow* could be defined as "traumatic realism": by reversing the chronology, Amis draws attention on the disruptions of time caused by trauma and on the effects of trauma on the contemporary age.

2.7 The significance of the time's reversal in *Time's Arrow*

The laws of physics tell us that heat flows from a warmer region to a cooler one, but not *vice versa*. The second law of thermodynamics describes the inescapable increase of entropy (that is, the amount of energy that is unusable because it has already flowed to the cooler region and cannot flow back) in closed physical systems. The British physicist A.S. Eddington coined the expression "time's arrow" to indicate the "one-way property of time"[296]. Eddington accorded to the second law of thermodynamics primacy among the

---

[295] M. Rothberg, *Traumatic Realism*, p. 21.
[296] A. S. Eddington, *The Nature of the Physical World*, Cambridge: Cambridge University Press, 1928, p. 69.

laws of physics: the increase of entropy describes the asymmetry of time and sets its direction.

In an interview with Margaret Reynolds, Martin Amis declared:

> It's not a totally fanciful notion to turn back, to reverse the arrow of time, because certain theories now exploded about the fate of the universe include this idea of the big crunch when everything has been flung out by the big bang, but then the explosive force of that thrust weakens, and then gravity starts to pull everything back in. And many physicists have theorized about the possibility of time going backwards in that event.[297]

Time's Arrow represents Amis's attempt to subvert the laws of physics by reversing the chronological order of the narrative. The very title of the novel refers to the flow of time, to the asymmetry that gives time a direction and that Amis's narrative structure undermines. In fact, the sequence of events in the novel runs opposite to our normal perception of time. As Maya Slater observed[298], Amis takes up the challenge posed by Nabokov in *Look at the Harlequins!*: "Nobody can imagine in physical terms the act of reversing the order of time. Time is not reversible"[299].

At the beginning of the novel, even words are momentarily reversed:

> "Dug. Dug" says the lady in the pharmacy.
> "Dug" I join in. "Oo y'rrah?"
> "Aid ut oo y'rrah?" (14)

However, after this initial demonstration the narrator helpfully starts translating for the reader: although conversations run backwards, the single words and sentences are conventionally written forward.

In a traditional narrative structure, the reader experiences the gradual unfolding of the plot. In *Time's Arrow*, Amis deconstructs this experience by resisting the directionality of time and altering its flow. Thereby, he manipulates our common perception of time and disorients us, throwing our intuitions into disarray. The disruption of causality and continuity leaves the reader in the same condition as a traumatized individual who cannot transform his or her traumatic memory into a coherent narrative. The backward temporality exposes the artificiality of time in chronologically ordered narratives, revealing how

---

[297] M. Amis, in M. Reynolds, *Martin Amis: The Essential Guide*, London: Vintage, 2003, p. 19.
[298] M. Slater, "Problems when Time Moves Backwards: Martin Amis's *Time's Arrow*", *English: The Journal of the English Association* 42.173 (1993), p. 141.
[299] V. Nabokov, *Look at the Harlequins!*, in V. Nabokov, *Novels 1969-1974*, New York: The Library of America, 1996, p. 746.

"normal", forward temporality is nothing but a convention. Moreover, it presents us with a conception of history and fiction as human constructs.

"Time is heading on towards something. It pours past unpreventably" (67): in *Time's Arrow*, everything leads to the past, which is unchangeable. According to the narrator's skewed perspective, this means that "[t]he future always comes true" (162). The reader does not see a character in a process of developing, but one who cannot change the course of his life, because his future is an "already-made past"[300]: everything has already happened and "must be played out, in reverse, scene by scene"[301].

The time's reversal denotes unending trauma and burdens the narrator with an already determined future that cannot be changed, but only experienced like a movie running backwards: an action which was originally freely chosen becomes the only action possible. This suggests the idea that the Holocaust is the climax of a catastrophic trajectory, the inevitable consequence of Europe's racist legacy: history appears as inescapable as the second law of thermodynamics[302]. At the end of the novel, where time seems to resume its forward direction, this idea is further reinforced:

> When Odilo closes his eyes I see an arrow fly – but wrongly. Point-first. Oh no, but then... We're away once more, over the field. Odilo Unverdorben and his eager heart. And I within, who came at the wrong time – either too soon, or after it was all too late. (173)

Amis's novel symbolizes the disarticulation of time caused by the Holocaust. The narrator's description of the painted clock at the railway station in Treblinka suggests that during the Holocaust time had no arrow. The painted clock is a clear metaphor of the Nazis' deceptive treatment of time, which in turn reflects the distortions of language, logic and morality during the Third Reich:

> There were signs and so on [...] and a clock. Every station, every journey, needs a clock. When we passed it, on our way to inspect the gravel pits, the big hand was on twelve and the little hand was on four. Which was incorrect! An error, a mistake: it was exactly 13:27. But we passed again, later, and the hands hadn't moved to an earlier time. Beneath the clock was an enormous arrow, on which was printed: Change Here For Eastern Trains. But time had no arrow, not here. (151)

---

[300] J. Brendle, "Forward to the Past: History and the Reversed Chronology Narrative in Martin Amis's *Time's Arrow*", *The American Journal of Semiotic* 12.1 (1995), p. 432.
[301] *Ibid.*, p. 427.
[302] R. Menke, "Narrative Reversal and the Thermodynamics of History in Martin Amis's *Time's Arrow*", *Modern Fiction Studies* 44.4 (1998), p. 973.

In the chronologically and logically reversed world of *Time's Arrow*, objects emerge intact and ready for use from the incinerator, the car crash, the garbage truck, and especially from the toilet: "[a]ll life, [...] all sustenance, all meaning [...] issue from a single household appliance: the toilet handle" (18). Every day, Tod takes the newspaper to the store, and the dateline "goes like this. After October 2, you get October 1. After October 1, you get September 30" (16). Food flows from toilet and trash to stomach to plate, until Tod returns it to the store, where he gets "generously reimbursed" for his pain (19). Garbage men "come sadly at morning" dispensing rubbish (51), and housemaids enter a spotless home, dirty all dishes, then drop money on the counter and leave (102).

"People all have jobs now, at the steel mill and the auto plant" (57), the narrator observes. Things gets cheaper and cheaper (46), cars become slower and less efficient (98), and Tod exchanges his colour TV for a black-and-white one (98). Children grow smaller and then enter hospitals from which they never return (41), while the old become healthier and stronger (15). Doctors spend their time wounding patients until they are healed by an accident or disease (85), cars have "five reverse gears and only one for forward" (30), and Hollywood movies dismantle couples (46).

The effects of the time's reversal are funny at first. For example:

> The business with the yellow cabs, it surely looks like an unimprovable deal. They're always there when you need one, even in the rain or when the theatres are closing. They pay you up front, no questions asked. They always know where you're going. They're great. No wonder we stand there, for hours on end, waving goodbye, or saluting – saluting this fine service. [...] Just the one hitch: they're always taking me places where I don't want to go. (74)

Furthermore, the narrator observes how tennis "is a pretty dumb game": "the fuzzy ball jumps out of the net, or out of the chicken wire at the back of the court, and the four of us bat it around until it is pocketed – quite arbitrarily, it seems to me – by the server" (20-1). He also has a difficult time understanding other facets of Tod's life, such as the fact that he takes toys and candy from children and returns them to the store for "[a] couple of bucks" (22-3), or the fact that he removes big bills from the collection plate on Sundays (23). Correspondence likewise is weird: Tod creates letters from ashes in the fire, unfolds them, and then mails them to the authors (23). Eating out is a rather bewildering ritual too: "Rounding it off with a cocktail, we finish our meal and sit there doggedly describing it to the waiter, with the menu there to jog our memory" (61).

Even the development of Tod's love affairs, described backwards, appears quite unusual: he collects someone's letter or photo from the trash or the fire, then they have a fight, followed by a relationship and sometimes sex, before Tod tries to seduce the woman, until she finally disappears from his life after a last meeting, usually "in the consulting rooms of Associated Medical Services" (65). The narrator is also surprised when he sees "[a] child's breathless wailing calmed by the firm slap of the father's hand", or "a dead ant revived by the careless press of a passing sole", or "a wounded finger healed and sealed by the knife blade". Likewise, he is amazed that Tod gradually gains strength, hair, and increased sexual energy, but "Tod doesn't appreciate the improvement" (36).

The novel's backwards narration completely alters causality, so that creation becomes destruction and healing becomes injuring. Tod spends years draining and crushing the tulips and roses of his beautiful garden:

> The garden was heaven when we started out, but over the years, well, don't blame me is all I'm saying. It wasn't my decision. It never is. [...] Look at it. A nightmare of wilt and mildew, of fungus and blackspot. All the tulips and roses he patiently drained and crushed, then sealed their exhumed corpses and took them in the paper bag to the store for money. All the weeds and nettles he screwed into the soil [...]. Such, then, are the fruits of Tod's meticulous vandalism. (26)

Run in reverse, gardening appears as the careful act of ruining the vegetation of a once-flourishing garden. Hence, the narrator concludes that "destruction – is difficult. Destruction is slow", while "creation [...] is no trouble at all" (26). This scene can be interpreted as a metaphor of the Nazi "healing-killing paradox", which inverted creation and destruction: comic reversals become tragic in such allegorical events.

The Nazi doctors' reversal of the medicine's goal, from healing to killing, is further symbolized in Amis's novel by the narrator's understanding of medical practice: according to him, medical work involves an endless fight "against health, against life and love" (103). Early in the novel, the narrator describes the fate of women in crisis centers:

> The women at the crisis centres and the refugees are all hiding from their redeemers. The crisis centre is not called a crisis centre for nothing. If you want a crisis, just check in. The welts, the abrasions and the black eyes get starker, more livid, until it is time for the women to return, in an ecstasy of distress, to the men who will suddenly heal them. (39)

Similarly, babies are taken to the hospital,

> and they're well enough, and you look them over and say something like "This little fella's just fine". And you're always dead wrong. Always. A day or two later the baby will be back, crimson-eared, or whoofing with croup. And you never do a damn thing for them. (53)

Doctors injure healthy patients, cover them in blood, and send them off howling in pain:

> Some guy comes in with a bandage around his head. We don't mess about. We'll soon have that off. He's got a hole in his head. So what do we do. We stick a nail in it. Get the nail – a good rusty one – from the trash or wherever. And lead him out to the Waiting Room where he's allowed to linger and holler for a while before we ferry him back to the night. (85)

"Because I am a healer, everything I do heals" (86) claims the narrator: in the name of healing, doctors commit atrocity upon atrocity. Therefore,

> the hospital is an atrocity-producing situation. Atrocity will follow atrocity, unstoppably. As if fresh atrocity were necessary to validate the atrocity that came before. As if the atrocity that came before was necessary to validate the atrocity that will come after. [...] Atrocity upon atrocity, and then more atrocity, and then more. (102)

This passage mirrors Lifton's characterization of Auschwitz as "an atrocity-producing situation"[303] and represents a darkly ironic parody of what Nazi doctors actually did at Auschwitz. Seen backwards, Tod's work as a doctor in America bears an uncanny and horrible resemblance to the work of Nazi doctors in the camps. The attentive reader should be able to identify this resemblance as a trigger trope anticipating Tod's role at Auschwitz.

Furthermore, the narrator's claim that "work liberates" when he sees how people on Friday evenings cheerfully prepare to begin the week (57) echoes the Nazi expression "Arbeit macht frei", resonating very much as the inscription over the gates of Auschwitz. The narrator will actually quote the inscription later on, when he arrives at Auschwitz: "'Arbeit Macht Frei' says the sign on the gate, with typically gruff and undesigning eloquence. The men work for their freedom" (131). Here, the narrator's words and the Nazis' reversed logic and language come uncomfortably close together and show how the Nazi language only makes sense in a reversed world. The appearance of the expression "work liberates" early in the novel anticipates to the attentive reader the narrator's "future" involvement in the Holocaust, working as a trigger trope.

Another trigger trope in *Time's Arrow* is represented by the narrator's conception of birth: babies vanish after a long goodbye. The narrator wonders: "Where do they disappear to?". But he immediately adds: "Don't ask that question. Never ask it. It's none of your business" (41). Similarly, when he notes that "[t]he insane have been taken off the street", he states: "we don't ask where

---

[303] R. J. Lifton, *The Nazi Doctors*, p. 425.

they've disappeared to. Never ask. It's better if you never ask" (57). These claims suggest a comparison with the false naivety of Holocaust bystanders.

The formal construction of Amis's novel is inextricably linked to its subject matter. The Holocaust is not simply an extreme instance of something that looks very strange backwards: "the text itself implies that the reason for the backwards narration is the 'time out of joint' of the Holocaust"[304]. Through the fictional device of the time's reversal, Amis exposes the atrocity of the Nazi ideology: the chronologically reversed form reflects the morally reversed content. In adapting to the crazy logic of a reversed narrative, the reader develops coping strategies to confront the inverted world of Auschwitz and to understand the obscenity of its logic.

In *Admitting the Holocaust*, Lawrence Langer states:

> Kierkegaard wrote somewhere that life is lived forward and understood backward [...] But just the opposite is true for the Holocaust experience: we live it backward in time, and once we arrive there, we find ourselves mired in its atrocities, a kind of historical quicksand that hinders our bid to bring it forward again into a meaningful future.[305]

Time's Arrow performs Langer's argument almost literally: through the time's reversal and the narrator's distorted perspective, Amis shows precisely how the Holocaust is lived backward and understood forward. In the novel, events always precede causes, and we read what has happened before knowing the reasons why it happened. As the narrator notes, "[o]ne thing led to another – actually it was more like the other way round" (56).

Langer's statement is further amplified by the narrator's claim that "[t]he world is going to start making sense" (124) when he approaches Auschwitz. Only in a reversed world can the Holocaust appear as morally acceptable: seen backwards, the death camp makes sense to the narrator, ovens of death become ovens of rebirth, and the destruction of the Jews becomes creation. "Our preternatural purpose? To dream a race. To make a people from the weather. From thunder and from lightning. With gas, with electricity, with shit, with fire" (128).

In a grotesque reversal of the process of genocide, people are restored to life by the infernal methods used to destroy them, providing what Diedrick calls "poetic justice – on a grand historical scale"[306]. Auschwitz produces whole

---

[304] S. Vice, "Formal Matters: Martin Amis, *Time's Arrow*", in S. Vice, *Holocaust Fiction*, London, New York: Routledge, 2000, p. 11.

[305] L. L. Langer, *Admitting the Holocaust: Collected Essays*, New York: Oxford University Press, 1996, p. 6.

[306] J. Diedrick, *Understanding Martin Amis*, p. 133.

trainloads of Jews, who are then provided with clothes that fit perfectly and united with their loved ones in tearful "familial unions and arranged marriages" (131): just as Hollywood dismantles fictional couples, Auschwitz creates real ones. When the camp is broken up, Jews are "deconcentrated" and "channelled back into society", then the ghettos are "dismantled and dispersed" (149), and Jews gradually gain more and more liberties, until they are finally diffused throughout Europe (164).

By inverting the arrow of time and the morality of Auschwitz, Amis defamiliarizes the Holocaust and presents us with a new perspective to think about its awfulness. The narrative is morally as well as chronologically turned around, so that the genocide appears as altruistic: the cruelty and destruction, apparently disguised, are actually highlighted by the strategy of the time's reversal, which reveals the anti-logic of the Holocaust. Amis underlines the moral significance of the novel's reversed chronology by claiming:

> The Holocaust would have been exactly what the Nazis said it was – i.e., a biomedical initiative for the cleansing of Germany – if, and only if, the arrow of time ran the other way. That's how fundamental the error was. And I think the novel expresses that.[307]

Time's reversal, memory and identity

Trauma is an experience of extreme deracination that annihilates the sense of continuity in one's life and disrupts memory and identity. *Time's Arrow*, by representing and mimicking the fragmentation of a traumatized psyche, can expand our understanding of traumatic memory and subjectivity. In particular, Amis raises questions about the authenticity of memory, its inevitable subjectivity, and its effects upon identity.

As Amis shows in the novel, memory is not a straightforward process of storage and retrieval: what an individual perceives as a memory of the past is in fact the subjective construction of past events in the present. The stories we narrate to others, and even to ourselves, are continually rewritten according to our needs and goals. Hence, memory is subject to distortions, omissions and falsifications, and cannot warranty an authentic representation of the past: "what and how one remembers depends much more on current cognitive structures than on (the original) past experiences"[308].

The narrator of *Time's Arrow*, living the protagonist's life backwards, has no memory of the past: he shares the protagonist's emotions, but not his memories and thoughts. If the arrow of time runs backwards, there can be no remembering, but only instant forgetting, because the past is future and has not happened yet.

---

[307] M. Amis, in M. Reynolds, *Martin Amis: The Essential Guide*, p. 20.
[308] C. Henke, "Remembering Selves, Constructing Selves. Memory and Identity in Contemporary British Fiction", *Journal for the Study of British Cultures* 10.1 (2003), p. 80.

The time's reversal thus affects the narrator's perception of memory, which for him means forgetting: "forgetting, not as a process of erosion and waste, but as an activity" (89). He is surprised at the human capacity to forget: "What is it with them, the human beings? I suppose they remember what they want to remember" (89); "[e]veryone becomes more innocent, constantly forgetting" (99). The ironic tone of these comments will become clear if we interpret them the right way round:

> What the Nazi criminal Odilo Unverdorben, despite his threefold identity change, could not manage to achieve – an active, deliberate forgetting of the past, strictly speaking a contradiction in terms – is the inevitable norm in the narrator's inverted world.[309]

Amis's novel testifies to the importance of remembering: the narrator, having no memory, is unable to look onto his future, because the possibility of a future depends on our capacity to remember. The narrator accumulates his own memories as he lives Tod's life backwards: "He forgets. I remember" (162). But the time's reversal transforms memory into precognition. Accordingly, the narrator interprets Tod's recurrent dreams as nightmarish prophecies of the future, while they are actually Tod's haunting memories of his past deeds.

The novel represents America as "a good hiding place for a war criminal – a lotus-like land of attenuated memory where no one inquires about Unverdorben's past and few care about history"[310]. In America, Unverdorben "ages and dies in obscurity – but not in peace"[311]. He is haunted by his Nazi past, as the narrator's reports of his dreams reveal: "I bet they don't have the dream we have. The figure in the white coat and black boots. In his wake, a blizzard of wind and sleet, like a storm of human souls" (16). Tod's dreams act as anticipations for both narrator and reader: Amis is using the doctor's nightmares to prepare the reader for the Auschwitz section of the book.

Time's Arrow also portrays the crisis of an individual's identity. The time's reversal reveals Odilo's attempts at losing his memory and changing his identity, while the figure of the doubled protagonist-narrator shows the precariousness of identity under extreme, traumatic circumstances. In the course of his life, the protagonist tries to escape from his identity and make himself anew by changing names and places. He goes by the names of Tod Friendly, John Young, Hamilton de Souza, and Odilo Unverdorben, and lives in many places: New Jersey, New York, Portugal, and Germany. He also has a habit of crumpling and burning all evidence of the past, such as love letters and photos. Nonetheless, his Nazi past haunts him.

---

[309] *Ibid.*, p. 88.
[310] J. Diedrick, *Understanding Martin Amis*, p. 138.
[311] *Ibid.*

The novel shows the impossibility of fully discarding the memory of one's past, and thus one's identity. There can be no escape from memory and the past: "no wilful forgetting, no self-fashioning of identity will work"[312]. In fact, although the protagonist leads somewhat different lives in different places under different names, he still retains the identity and memories of the Nazi doctor Odilo Unverdorben: "The memory of his deeds, the marks of his former identity, cannot be cast off as can be his names. Identity is more than the effect of a change of name and location; it is, on the contrary, what one has become through time"[313].

The backwards narration symbolizes the impossibility of coming to terms with a haunting past. It also represents the protagonist's unrealizable wish to reverse time and undo history, or at least to exonerate himself of the memory of guilt by making his crimes appear morally right. By inverting the arrow of time, Amis makes the protagonist inevitably become the Nazi criminal he has been. Moreover, the ending of the novel with Odilo's birth suggests the possibility of "a reversal of the reversal, an endless repetition of forward-backward cycles of the protagonist's life"[314].

Like Benjamin's angel of history, Amis's narrator feels the past as always present: his face is turned toward the past, but his life is irresistibly propelled into the future[315]. According to Sara Horowitz, the narrator of *Time's Arrow* shares with Benjamin's angel of history the aspiration to reverse temporality and undo history. She argues that the narrator "restores and resurrects – and thus redeems history", while the angel is "unable to undo the catastrophe he continues to watch"[316]. However, although *Time's Arrow* reverses the flow of time, I think that the novel actually exposes the *impossibility* of undoing history: the backwards movement of the protagonist's doubled consciousness is counteracted by the inescapable forwards movement of the protagonist's body.

The redemptive capacity of the narrator is a chimera: his actions have been predetermined by Tod's previous actions. Like Benjamin's angel, Amis's narrator can only follow. *Time's Arrow* thus reveals that the human desire to overcome time and relive life all over again cannot be fulfilled. Paradoxically, precisely by reversing the arrow of time Amis confirms Heraclitus's assertion that the past is unrepeatable, because all things go: "you cannot step into the same river twice, for other waters are ever flowing on to you"[317].

---

[312] C. Henke, "Remembering Selves", p. 90.
[313] *Ibid.*, p. 88.
[314] *Ibid.*, p. 90.
[315] W. Benjamin, "Theses on the Philosophy of History", in W. Benjamin, *Illuminations*, trans. H. Zohn, New York: Schocken Books, 1988, pp. 257-8.
[316] S. Horowitz, *Voicing the Void: Muteness and Memory in Holocaust Fiction*. Albany: State University of New York Press, 1997, p. 194.
[317] Heraclitus, *Fragment 41*.

2.8 The status of the narrator in *Time's Arrow*

The narrative voice has great importance in *Time's Arrow*. The narrator defines himself as a "passenger or parasite" (16) within the protagonist's body, but at the same time he is divorced from it: he is the dissociated part of the protagonist's self. The consciousness-split occurs at the beginning of the novel: at the moment of his death, Tod Friendly "'gives birth' to a *Doppelgänger* (literally, 'double-goer')"[318], a separated self who starts narrating Tod's life in reverse.

The narrator gradually becomes aware of the separation and realizes that he has no control over the body he inhabits: "Something isn't quite working: this body I'm in won't take orders from this will of mine. Look around, I say. But his neck ignores me. His eyes have their own agenda" (13). He feels he lives in a special world that he cannot fully understand, and wonders:

> Why am I walking *backwards* into the house? Wait. Is it dusk coming, or is it dawn? What is the – what is the sequence of the journey I'm on? What are its rules? Why are the birds singing so strangely? Where am I heading? (14)

Moreover, the narrator possesses "a fair amount of value-free information, or general knowledge", "a superb vocabulary", and "a nonchalant command of all grammatical rules" (16). However, he does not fully understand that his backward trajectory through time violates ordinary chronology. He has "no name and no body" (155), nor access to Tod's memory, but he can feel his emotions and experience his bodily sensations: "I have no access to his thoughts – but I am awash with his emotions" (15).

Thanks to this peculiar status of the narrator, the reader is left unaware of Tod's secret and of his past, allowing for a suspense that would otherwise be impossible in an "autobiography" narrated backwards. The narrator is an "eyewitness" who replicates the reader's experience, but he is unreliable. In fact, our knowledge is often superior to his: "For the narrator, this is how the world is. It's an innocent narrator. [...] all the moral work has to be done by the reader. [...] it's the reader, not the narrator, who is dealing with the morality"[319].

In the same way as the time's reversal, the particular status of the narrator is not simply a formal device: the form of the novel has an important role in shaping the content and its reception. The fact that the narrator applies a forward logic to a backward world makes him unable to express and interpret properly

---

[318] J. Diedrick, *Undestanding Martin Amis*, p.133.
[319] M. Amis, in D. Weich, "Old Martin Amis Is in Your Face Again", *Powell's Author Interviews*, Nov 2003, <http://www.powells.com/authors/amis.html>.

what is happening, and to provide moral judgments. He feels that something is wrong with him:

> I puzzle a lot, if the truth be known. In fact I've had to conclude that I am generally rather slow on the uptake. Possibly even subnormal, or mildly autistic. It may very well be that I'm not playing with a full deck. The cards won't add up for me; the world won't start making sense. (37)

The narrator continuously misreads signs and misinterprets events, so that readers are forced to read between the lines and reflect upon the narrator's words. The narrator's difficulties at understanding and describing the topsy-turvy world in which he lives reveal the inappropriateness of language for representing a post-traumatic world. Furthermore, the bifurcation of perspectives raises questions about agency, insofar as it problematizes the assigning of responsibility and encourages the reader to consider to what degree Odilo and the narrator have freedom to act.

As we have seen, Amis's narrator represents a fictionalization of the Nazi doctors' psychological profile, which is characterized by processes of psychic numbing and doubling, and by mechanisms of disavowal and derealization. In particular, the split between Odilo and the narrator reflects the psychological doubling of the Nazi doctors: although the narrator defines himself as a passenger in Tod's head, in reality he *is* Tod. His ignorance of this state of affairs represents the partly unconscious nature of the process of doubling.

The doubled self of the protagonist creates a split between two points of view: we see through Tod's eyes, but we only have access to the narrator's interpretation of what we see. What is counter-intuitive for the narrator is actually the intuitive world for his double: "Tod is sane, apparently, and his world is shared. It just seems to me that the film is running backwards" (16). Because of this doubled-perspective, readers cannot rely on the narrator and must apply their own moral values in order to judge what is happening and give meaning to the otherwise meaningless sequence of events presented by the narrator.

The reader has to mediate between two points of view, none of which is entirely reliable: on the one hand, he or she sees the protagonist's actions and reactions, and, on the other, Tod's interpretations of them. One of the protagonist's names, "Unverdorben", encapsulates the dual structure of his self: in German, *unverdorben* means depraved, corrupt, while *verdorben* is its antonym, meaning innocent, unspoilt. Hence, the name "Unverdorben" encloses in itself both the protagonist and his double, the doctor's "Auschwitz-self" and his "pre-war self".

Having no access to the protagonist's thoughts, the narrator does not know how the protagonist himself perceives what is happening: he can only see a series of events, without any of the thoughts behind them, and thus reaches wrong conclusions. In the same way as a historian, he is attempting to reconstruct a true past from a series of clues: not unlike Amis's narrator, the historian discovers facts and arranges them to tell a story, often missing the reasons why people acted in that way, or noticing things that the protagonists ignored.

Throughout the text, the narrator's use of personal pronouns shifts from the first person to the third person, indicating his ambiguous and fluctuant relationship with the protagonist. The use of the third person is a manifestation of Lifton's insight that the Nazi doctors he interviewed "could examine events in considerable detail [...] but almost in the manner of a third person"[320]. As Amis's narrator, Lifton's Nazi doctors were, morally speaking, "not quite present": "none of them – not a single former Nazi doctor I spoke to – arrived at a clear ethical evaluation of what he had done, and what he had been part of"[321].

Similarly, by refusing to acknowledge Tod's body as his own, the narrator is able to reject his involvement and responsibility in what he believes to be the atrocities committed in American hospitals. He holds the "other entity", Tod's body, responsible for the inhumane acts they are committing: "I'm glad it's not my body that is actually touching their bodies. I'm glad I have *his* body, in between" (102).

The narrator becomes much more closely involved with his other self at Auschwitz, where Odilo's two selves are reconciled. When he arrives at Auschwitz, the narrator announces himself as "I, Odilo Unverdorben" (124), without the pronominal distinction that had previously marked his separation from Tod: narrator and protagonist are "one now, fused for a preternatural purpose" (124). Seen backwards, the process of doubling becomes the reconciliation of two separate selves. After the war and the killings end, the world stops making sense and the narrator goes back to the third person: "Odilo forgets everything again" (157).

In the Auschwitz section, the narrator is even more unreliable than in the first part of the novel: he shares Odilo's point of view and approves of his behaviour. He no longer comments on the backwardness of the world, but simply describes Auschwitz and even believes in its topsy-turvy logic: since things run backwards, killing becomes healing and genocide becomes genesis, so that the death camps appear as places where life is created from waste. Therefore, the atrocities of Auschwitz make perfect sense to the narrator, who is proud of his involvement in the "creation" of the Jews:

---

[320] R. J. Lifton, *The Nazi Doctors*, p. 8.
[321] *Ibid*.

> The patients, still dead, were delivered out on a stretcher-like apparatus. [...] Thence to the Chamber, where the bodies were stacked carefully [...] There was usually a long wait while the gas was invisibly introduced by the ventilation grills. [...] I always felt a gorgeous relief at the moment of the first stirring. [...] It was I, Odilo Unverdorben, who personally removed the pellets of Zyklon B and entrusted them to the pharmacist in his white coat. [...] Clothes, spectacles, hair, spinal braces and so on – these came later. Entirely intelligibly, though, to prevent needless suffering, the dental work was usually completed while the patients were not yet alive. (129)

The narrator sees Auschwitz as a triumph of the human power to create: "violence creates, here on earth. Never before have we been so potent" (158). At the expense of the intelligibility of everything else, he has made sense of the Holocaust. He considers his job as a morally good duty and does not understand why Herta, his wife, thinks that what the Nazis are doing is illegal:

> My wife Herta paid her first visit to Auschwitz in the spring of 1944, which was perhaps unfortunate: we were then doing the Hungarian Jews, and at an incredible rate, something like 10,000 a day. [...] I [...] got the distinct impression that Herta disapproves of the work I am doing here. [...] In one of her baffling letters Herta goes so far as to question the *legality* of the work we are doing here. (137-142)

The narrator judges what he experiences on the basis of his past, which is Odilo's future, and describes the atrocities of Auschwitz in the same cheerful and humorous manner as other events in Tod's life. At Auschwitz, life suddenly makes sense to him, and his medical work now appears to him beneficial. The narrator's pretended innocence, his misunderstanding of what he is actually doing, and his celebration of the atrocities committed at Auschwitz make the narrative more and more shocking for the reader, who keeps reversing backward time into forward time and knows that what is happening is actually horrible.

The two most striking narrative features of *Time's Arrow* – the time's reversal and the particular status of the narrator – are closely linked. A clear instance of this link is provided by the selection scene:

> These familial unions and arranged marriages, known as selections on the ramp, were the regular highpoints of the KZ routine. [...] As matchmakers, we didn't know the meaning of the word failure; on the ramps, stunning successes were as cheap as spit. When the families coalesced, how their hands and eyes would plead for one another, under our indulgent gaze. (131-2)

Because he sees them backwards, the narrator interprets the selections as scenes of reconciliation and joy and does not recognize the moral atrocity of what he is describing: to him, Odilo's crimes appear as morally right. He has activated the mechanisms of disavowal and derealization described by Lifton: "The Nazi doctor knew that he selected, but did not interpret selection as murder"[322]. The narrator has even appropriated the rhetoric of Nazi militarism: "this was our mission after all: to make Germany whole. To heal her wounds and make her whole" (149).

2.9 The role of the reader in *Time's Arrow*

In trauma fiction, the novel's impact on the reader is often more important than the accuracy of the facts narrated: *Time's Arrow* is no exception in this respect, having an evidently performative function. Its goal is to move and wound the audience, to overcome the desensitization of readers, and to render the uniqueness and incomprehensibility of trauma without neutralizing its impact. Readers should leave behind any sense of expectation and abandon any reliance on the possibility of arriving at a conclusion in the traditional sense: they are left wandering through the text, which must be approached thoughtfully, worked at, and decoded.

The role of the reader in *Time's Arrow* is an active one: he or she cannot rely upon the guiding hand of the author. Amis does not allow us to be passive spectators, but requires an ethically engaged and active response: "You present it as a miracle, but the reader is supplying all the tragedy"[323]. *Time's Arrow* does not provide readers with comfort and consolation, but immerses them in the horror of the Holocaust and demands self-reflection, moral reckoning and social action, thereby favouring a new approach not only to the Holocaust, but also to contemporary societies and cultures.

The reader of *Time's Arrow* faces a complex ethical situation: Amis initially entices us to sympathize and even identify with the protagonist, only to tell us later that he has been a Nazi doctor. Upon revelation of the protagonist's secret trauma and identity, the reader's interpretation of what he or she has been reading changes radically. The ironic approach challenges our notion of what is acceptable in Holocaust representation. However, it does not trivialize the Holocaust, but draws the reader into it by using humor to lower his or her guard against horror: satire and the grotesque combine with a tragic subject to break down our resistance to horror.

Time's Arrow invites us to get closer to the Holocaust without our being aware that we are doing it. By denying us distance from the Holocaust, Amis

---

[322] *Ibid.*, p. 422.
[323] M. Amis, in J. Diedrick, *Understanding Martin Amis*, p. 134.

confronts us with a violent force in history that we are encouraged to resist, but in which we are inevitably implicated.

> Reading *Time's Arrow* can be an extremely disturbing experience. Some readers have complained that the cleverness and showiness of the time experiment detracts from the seriousness of the subject, but this need not be so. Read in the tradition of an experimental and historically traumatised novel [...] the disturbances created by the novel's form and by its horrendous subject matter hang nightmarishly together.[324]

Portraying a perpetrator's trauma does not imply erasing the difference between victim and perpetrator: instead, it offers us a unique and particular perspective on the circumstances that made the Holocaust possible. The reader is forced to look anew at the horrors of history and to re-consider his or her own position of responsibility. Being written backwards, and from the point of view of a Nazi doctor, *Time's Arrow* avoids the desensitization that might derive from the proliferation of survivors' testimonies and from the routinization of "[t]he idiom of violence"[325]. It creates cognitive and emotional dissonance and brings the reader inside the events, asking him or her to respond to the horror of the Holocaust in an ethically engaged way.

Time's Arrow problematizes the position of the reader, who is forced to negotiate a pathway of responsiveness and responsibility and to reflect upon his or her own involvement in evil. Its narrative strategies engage the reader, implicating him or her in the horror of the Holocaust, and call for "a mixed response that often combines identification, revulsion and judgment"[326]. Amis places special demands on his readers:

> The reader has to do all the morality, because these terrible events are described as benevolent, but also in such a way that, I hope, there is a sort of disgust and an unreality and self-delusion in the way it's shown. He keeps wondering why it has to be so ugly, this essentially benevolent action, why it is so filthy and ugly. It was a coprocentric universe. They called Auschwitz "anus mundi". So it's there, but the narrator can't spot it, the *reader* has to do all that.[327]

In the first part of the novel, the reader is drawn into the story and made sympathetic with the narrator. The need for understanding links reader and narrator: they share the same confusion about Tod's past. The questions asked

---

[324] R. Brown, "Martin Amis: Overview", in L. Henderson (ed.), *Contemporary Novelists*, London: St. James's Press, 1991, p. 36.
[325] G. Hartman, *The Longest Shadow*, p. 85.
[326] J. Diedrick, *Understanding Martin Amis*, p. 27.
[327] M. Amis, in M. Reynolds, *Martin Amis: The Essential Guide*, p. 21.

by the narrator are the same that the reader too wants answered: "What [does] the secret have to do with?" (12), "Why am I walking *backwards* into the house? [...] what is the sequence of the journey I'm on? [...] Where am I heading?" (14), "Where does the dream come from?" (48).

Hence, Amis's narrative strategy compels the reader to identify with the narrator's attempts at making sense of Tod's puzzling behaviour. When we discover Tod's terrible secret, we feel guilty for our previous sympathy towards the narrator, who is his doubled self, and we are shocked by the fact that he does not express horror at the systematic brutality around him: the narrator's distorted perspective and his lack of morality increase the reader's horror.

Moreover, readers are forced to share the misperceptions of the narrator, whose traumatized and distorted point of view obscures our comprehension of the events. Yet, there is a gap between the narrator's misunderstandings and what the reader understands, because the reader can judge what the narrator cannot. In fact, being familiar with the forward passage of time, we understand almost immediately that time is running backwards and that the narrator's judgments are flawed: what the narrator describes is not what is actually happening. As a consequence, it is the reader who has the responsibility to create the meaning of the narrative by going beyond the surface and piecing together the veiled clues that obliquely reveal "Tod's cruelty, his secret" (40). This implicates the reader in the discovery of horrors he or she already knows but must acknowledge again.

Amis invites the reader to distrust the narrator and encourages us to suspect his judgments: we soon learn that we cannot rely on the narrator, because his inverted sense of time leads to a reversal of logic and morality. The ironic distance between the narrator's account and the reader's understanding is greatest as Tod begins his work at Auschwitz and claims that "[t]he world, after all, here in Auschwitz, has a new habit. It makes sense" (138): the narrator's positive response to the death camp shocks the reader, who knows that the reality of Auschwitz, seen the right way round, makes no sense at all.

As readers of *Time's Arrow*, we are required certain skills: we should be able to perceive the discrepancy between what is said explicitly and what is left unsaid, and to provide the unwritten part of the text. The reader has to be active, to become a *wreader,* that is, both reader and writer, fully involved in the creation of the text's meaning. We must continually reverse the narrative sequence and imagine the antithesis of the narrator's interpretations of events in order to understand his account and reconstruct the story. This forces us to assume a position of agency in the narrative as well as in history, and to recognize our responsibility and admit that we are not innocent: Amis places us in the same position as those bystanders who knew what was happening at Auschwitz and did nothing to avoid or stop it.

The discrepancy between the narrator's discourse and the reader's understanding is further enhanced by the strategy of the time's reversal. We must constantly be on our guard, continually reconstructing into a forward chronology what the narrator relates in reverse and translating the backward processes, plotlines and conversations into normal time.

> Amis, by reversing the order of events, has deprived us of our ease of reading. We can no longer read casually, because the mass of what we normally take for granted as readers has been swept away. Our only defence is not to let our guard slip, not to let anything pass without scrutinizing it first. Proof-readers seeking out errors sometimes find it helpful to read a text backwards: they can concentrate on each individual word without allowing their eye to run on to the next. Amis, by reversing the text before we ever get to it, has turned us all into proof-readers of his novel.[328]

The time's reversal puts the reader in a very curious position, making him or her stumble along through the narrative in the attempt to unravel the plot and make sense of what he or she is being shown. The "sinister reversal" (54) of conventional chronological order encourages an active response from the reader, and demands that he or she mentally reverses the plot to assemble the *fabula*.

In the same way as Dori Laub's ideal listener of traumatized testimonies, the reader of *Time's Arrow*, following a "journey fraught with dangers", must be "unobtrusively [...] yet imminently present, active, in the lead" so that "when the flow of fragments falters" he or she has to "enhance them and induce their free expression"[329]. It is precisely this cognitive and emotional engagement required by Amis's novel that takes readers closer to trauma and allows them to understand it from within.

During the first part of the novel, readers gradually become adjusted to an inverted world where results precede actions, and gain a habit of interpreting backwards what they are reading: this prepares them for the Auschwitz section, inducing alertness and protecting them from falling into a morally reversed interpretation. Moreover, *Time's Arrow* makes us realize how easily we have been desensitized and grown accustomed to atrocity: when we see the protagonist committing horrible crimes at Auschwitz, we are horrified and shocked to be able to accept this atrocity, and we feel guilty for our reactions. The reader is disturbed by the irony that results from the reversal of time, which challenges the reader's perception of what is possible in a supposedly rational world. The role and reactions of the reader are thus influenced by the fact the time runs backwards.

---

[328] M. Slater, "Problems when Time Moves Backwards", p. 142.
[329] D. Laub, "Bearing Witness, or the Vicissitudes of Listening", in S. Felman and D. Laub, *Testimony*, pp. 71-2.

The time's reversal sets the reader another challenge by causing a reversal of the usual contract between novelist and reader. As the narrative progresses, we increasingly realize that we cannot measure what we learn against what has happened so far in the narrative: we must wait to measure it against what is to come, continually re-evaluating "earlier" incidents in the light of "later" events. For example, the narrator repetitively alludes to Tod's dream of the "bomb baby" that exerts an incredible power over its parents (48, 55, 67, 135). This dream-image will acquire new significance later on, when a baby's cry gives away the hiding place of a Jewish family, so that Odilo discovers them: the explosive effect of the baby's cry is that it betrayed "thirty souls" to Unverdorben. The chronological reversal completely subverts the traditional process of forecasting: readers do not forecast what will happen in the future, but conjecture about the causes of the events that have already been presented.

The reversed chronology defamiliarizes the events of the Holocaust and produces an alienation effect: it makes the familiar look strange, so that the reader cannot view it with the same reflex banality caused by over-familiarity with conventional Holocaust narratives and is propelled into what Freud calls "the uncanny". The time's reversal demands the reader a more active and attentive engagement: in order to make sense of what is happening, readers must employ their own memory and knowledge.

Amis's novel thus requires an *uncommon reader*, one who is able to recognize the disjunction between the history of the Holocaust and the narrator's perverse version of it: otherwise, the text could not defamiliarize the Holocaust and implicate us in it. The reader must be an artist as well, fully responsive to the book, rewriting in the process of reading: as I have already noted, the reader becomes *wreader*. Amis defines a position of agency for the reader by encouraging us to move beyond the aesthetic value of the story and to examine our own potential complicity in evil: we are placed in a grey zone of moral uncertainty and ambiguity.

Time's Arrow presupposes and relies on the figure of the "reader-supposed-to-know"[330]: the ideal reader should be able and willing to draw on his or her own previous knowledge and moral values in order to interpret the story of the protagonist's life. For example, the trigger words – such as train, smoke, deport, gas, and shower – that Amis has spread along the narrative represent hints at what is to come: only an attentive and refined reader, who knows where these words come from, is able to recognize as narrative triggers.

Amis thwarts the reader's desire for a satisfactory solution, refusing to exorcise the atrocity in a rational explanation. Knowing that Tod's life has already been lived, the reader is not reading for the unfolding possibilities of Tod's life, but for the slow revelation of his ineluctable fate. The narrator's

---

[330] S. Vice, *Holocaust Fiction*, p. 35.

inability to exert control over Tod's body reinforces the reader's sense that the course of his life has already been determined. However, this does not imply that the reader should passively accept this atrocity as part of an irrational and chaotic world. Ironically, as he depicts a character incapable of resisting the Nazi ideology, Amis constructs a position of agency for the reader: in fact, the time's reversal and the narrator's twisted perspective increase the reader's horror and force him or her to be active.

CONCLUSION: "STYLE *IS* MORALITY"

Most of the negative criticism about *Time's Arrow* focuses on the subordination of content to form and on the inappropriateness of dealing with a subject so distressing and tragic as the Holocaust in a humorous, ironic, or satirical way, charging Amis with cynicism and lack of morality. For example, Pearl K. Bell describes *Time's Arrow* as a "grievously misguided approach to the Holocaust" and defines its narrative technique "a bag of tricks gamemanship"[331], claiming: "Such manipulative 'irony' denies the essential horror of Auschwitz. [...] Amis, [...] in violating the order of cause and effect, trivializes what he has exploited but failed to comprehend"[332]. Similarly, Buchan argues that Amis "exploit[s] the horror and glamour of Auschwitz [...] for literary fun and profit"[333].

In Holocaust Studies, humor has often been considered harmful, irresponsible and ethically ambiguous. However, *Time's Arrow* shows that humor can be an ethically appropriate mode for representing trauma. In an interview, Amis has claimed his conviction that humor is a fundamental aspect of human life, and that the ironic tone of *Time's Arrow* is not indecent:

> Nazism was a biomedical vision to excise the cancer of Jewry. To turn it into something that *creates* Jewry is a respectable irony. [...] you can only go near the subject in a sepulchral hush. [...] You cannot take away your sense of humour. [...] as Clive James once said, "Humour is just common sense dancing". And those who have no humour have no common sense either.[334]

As we have already seen, the use of irony and humor can serve the purpose of lowering the reader's guard against horror: "Satire and the grotesque combine to break down our normal resistance to aberration and hence to prepare us for depictions of the Holocaust in which aberration was the norm"[335]. Thus, humor can make horror more credible and bring readers close to it without their being aware that they are doing it.

According to Amis's detractors, his work exemplifies the worst that pop-culture has to offer: this is, more generally, the perspective that has been applied to postmodernism as a whole, which has been defined as "essentially depthless,

---

[331] P. K. Bell, "A review of *Time's Arrow*", *Partisan Review* 59.2 (1992), p. 285.
[332] *Ibid.*
[333] J. Buchan, "The return of Dr. Death", *The Spectator* 28 September 1991, p. 37.
[334] M. Amis, in M. Reynolds, *Martin Amis: The Essential Guide.*, p. 20.
[335] M. Cory, "Comedic Distance in Holocaust Literature", *Journal of American Culture* 18.1 (1995), p. 37.

trivial kitsch"[336]. However, Amis's postmodernism does not deny history nor morality. As Linda Hutcheon claims,

> [t]o challenge history or its writing is not to deny either [...] It is not that truth and reference have ceased to exist [...] it is that they have ceased to be unproblematic issues. We are not witnessing a degeneration into the hyperreal without origin or reality, but a questioning of what 'real' can mean and how we can know it.[337]

In *Time's Arrow*, morality is not denied, but challenged: traditional humanist and Enlightenment values are indeed criticized, twisted and contorted, but they are still part of Amis's novel. "If life has changed profoundly in the late twentieth century, it follows that the forms that represent life must change as well"[338]: as Amis put it, "[w]hat you're always looking for, is a way to see the world differently".[339] However, this does not mean that in the post-Holocaust era moral values must be completely erased or subverted: they are questioned and contested, and are no longer as clear as those defined by the Enlightenment, but they are still present and necessary.

The form and content are inseparable in *Time's Arrow*: by moving backwards in time, Amis's novel confronts the moral outrage of the Holocaust. Hence, Amis does not prioritize entertainment over morality: the time's reversal is not an experiment *per se*, but an attempt to transmit a moral content through form. For him, style and subject cannot be separated in literature: "Personally, I've always believed in the indivisibility of form and content. [...] Style is not neutral; it gives moral directions"[340]. And: "Style isn't something added on; it's intrinsic to the perceptions and the way you see life"[341].

The impossible reversal of time in Amis's novel reminds us that "something seemingly impossible turned out to be eminently possible"[342]: *Time's Arrow* is not an immoral novel, and its style is appropriate to the content. Amis's focus on style makes demands "on the thinking, analysing, feeling capacity of the

---

[336] L. Hutcheon, *A Poetics of Postmodernism*, London, New York: Routledge, 1988, p. 24. Here, Hutcheon is referring to the ideas expressed by Terry Eagleton and Fredric Jameson. See also T. Eagleton, "Capitalism, Modernism and Postmodernism", *New Left Review* 152 (1985): 60-73; and F. Jameson, "Postmodernism, Or The Cultural Logic of Late Capitalism", *New Left Review* 146 (1984): 53-92.
[337] *Ibid.*, p. 223.
[338] J. Diedrick, *Understanding Martin Amis.*, p. 21.
[339] *Ibid.*, p. 257, n. 1.
[340] M. Amis, in N. Caputo, "L'etica della forma: strategie di straniamento in *Other People: A Mystery Story* (1981) e *Time's Arrow* (1991) di Martin Amis", *Confronto letterario* 23 (1995), p. 74.
[341] M. Amis, in D. Weich , "Old Martin Amis Is in Your Face Again".
[342] N. Rosenfeld, "Turning Back: Retracing Twentieth-Century Trauma in Virginia Wolf, Martin Amis, and W. G. Sebald", *Partial Answers* 2.2 (2004), p. 125.

reader"[343]: it does not detach readers from the horrors of the Holocaust, but makes them reflect more deeply on it, thereby contributing to make them aware of the reversed logic governing the Nazi genocide.

Because time runs backwards and the narrator has no access to the protagonist's memory, we discover Tod's secret only towards the end of the novel: this shocks us, and compels us to reconsider our previous reactions and "our relation to the whole question of guilt, complicity and punishment"[344]. Through style, Amis manipulates our reactions, forcing us to reflect upon our moral responsibilities and leading us towards an ethically engaged interpretation of events. In fact, Amis's style has a moral purpose, as Amis himself underlined by claiming: "style *is* morality: morality detailed, configured, intensified. It's not in the mere narrative arrangement of good and bad that morality makes itself felt. It can be there in every sentence"[345].

The artfully contrived structure of *Time's Arrow* defamiliarizes the horror of the Holocaust and leaves the reader with an abiding uneasiness. The constant manufacturing of the uncanny makes the world appear strange and enthrals the reader with the transformation of the familiar into the unfamiliar. Thereby, *Time's Arrow* avoids desensitizing and anesthetizing readers and favours an active form of remembering. As Amis noted, "[t]hose images of the rail tracks and the smoke stacks and the terrible emaciated bodies are almost too familiar to us now. There has to be another route to Auschwitz"[346].

Indeed, Amis's experimental style has a moral purpose: as Diedrick put it, "the narrative conceit of *Time's Arrow* is placed wholly in the service of a grim moral reckoning"[347]. The time's reversal and the consequent inversion of causality are perfectly in keeping with the Nazis' reversed morality and thus implicitly warn us against turning logic upside down. The novel's ironic mode and its other stylistic devices dramatize the gap between conventional logic and the Holocaust: in particular, the narrator's misinterpretations and the reversal of time underline the topsy-turvy logic that made Nazi doctors choose destruction rather than creation, killing rather than healing.

By confronting the complex issue of the complicity among perpetrators and bystanders during the Nazi period, *Time's Arrow* reveals the importance of thinking actively and acting thoughtfully. Although thinking about the Holocaust cannot erase it nor undo its horrific reality, it could help us deconstruct, or at least expose, the forces of collaboration and complicity that made the implementation of the Nazi genocide possible.

---

[343] M. Reynolds, *Martin Amis: The Essential Guide*, p. 8.
[344] *Ibid.*
[345] M. Amis, *Experience: A Memoir*, New York: Miramax, 2000, p. 122.
[346] M. Amis, in D. Weich, "Old Martin Amis Is in Your Face Again".
[347] J. Diedrick, *Understanding Martin Amis*, p. 135.

In our post-traumatic culture, thinking about the Holocaust is a moral command: not to think about it is to act in complicity with the silence of those who stood by and did nothing. According to Hannah Arendt, it was precisely thoughtlessness that predisposed "average" people like Adolf Eichmann to become cruel perpetrators of atrocious crimes[348]. Similarly, Amis suggests that Odilo is thoughtless: he has surrendered his free will and reason in order to serve evil as a Nazi doctor. In fact, at the beginning of the novel the narrator notes: "I speak without volition, in the same way that I do everything else" (14).

Thoughtlessness and ideological manipulation are among Amis's satirical targets. When Tod arrives at Auschwitz, the narrator does not question the ideology he is ensconced in, he just follows: "[w]e ask no questions. Because here there is no why" (134). The narrator's lack of agency and thought is part of Amis's warning to readers about the dangers of complacency and thoughtlessness: through narrative form, Amis satirically points out that we must think autonomously and work actively to create a better world, if we are to avoid falling back into the horrors of the past.

Amis is concerned with the potential for evil that lies within all human beings. *Time's Arrow* implicates readers in the atrocity of the Holocaust by underlining the unexceptional nature of its Nazi doctor protagonist: "Odilo Unverdorben, as a moral being, is absolutely unexceptional" (164). Odilo is a typical product of his culture, "innocent, emotional, popular and stupid" (157). Notably, he is also susceptible to group mentality, which takes over individual thinking and the need to make moral decisions: "Odilo Unverdorben [...] is [...] liable to do what everybody else does, good or bad, with no limit, once under the cover of numbers. He could never be an exception" (164). Moreover, by underlining Odilo's "quiet dedication" (142) to the Nazi cause, Amis further emphasizes the fact that horrors such as the Holocaust were possible because of the efforts of ordinary, unremarkable people.

Therefore, *Time's Arrow* represents a warning: the fact that a trivial, average individual could "quietly dedicate" himself to genocide is frightening and compels us towards reflection, so that we are forced to recognize that we are all potential perpetrators. This awareness is disturbing, because it clarifies that "the Holocaust was a tragedy for the human spirit"[349] (although, of course, it was much more tragic for its direct victims). Only by acknowledging the possibility of our own involvement in evil and by resisting ideological manipulations can we prevent such atrocities from happening again: Amis's novel is a warning to the readers about the difficult but necessary work to counter the atavistic desire for final solutions.

---

[348] H. Arendt, *Eichmann in Jerusalem: A Report on the Banality of Evil*, New York: Penguin Books, 1994, pp. 287-8.
[349] S. Vice, *Holocaust Fiction*, p. 36.

The time's reversal destabilizes all conventions of mimesis and subverts the chronological order of traditional historical narratives, which explain a past event in a cause-effect sequence and may thus suggest that there is a *cause* for atrocity. These kinds of narratives reassure us that we have moved beyond the atrocities of the past, and that the forces that produced such atrocities have been conquered. On the contrary, Amis refuses to offer such reassurance, denying the reader any distance from the Holocaust and any comforting rationalization of it.

Time's Arrow can be considered as "trauma fiction" precisely because it testifies to an event that is not yet over. Amis places the reader, uncannily, between the tragic and the comic poles of experience, so that he or she is not quieted with awe in the face of atrocity, but forced to recognize the terrible continuity between past, present, and future. In particular, the strategy of the time's reversal challenges the very idea of a future which is able to overcome the past and reminds us that genocide can happen again at any time: chronological distance does not make the Holocaust less significant.

The structure of Amis's novel undercuts the positivistic faith in historical progress. Amis does not provide us with a secure moral basis from which to understand the events of the protagonist's life and of history. In fact, his concern is not explanation, but warning: he puts readers on guard by confronting them with a past event that is not solved and not explained by the narrative. The refusal to locate a cause for the Holocaust compels the reader to acknowledge that the event has not been understood, and that the forces that led to it have not been overcome. This awakens a sense of horror at the inexplicability of the Nazi past and avoids rendering readers morally numb to the atrocity of the Holocaust, by making them reflect on the lack of explanation for evil.

In *Time's Arrow*, aesthetic gratification serves the purpose of giving us a reason for reading a Holocaust novel, which might otherwise seem too unpleasant. Despite the fact that they are formally disguised and even undone by the narrative structure, the atrocity and destruction of the Holocaust are actually emphasized: the strategy of the time's reversal draws attention to the counter-intuitive nature of Nazi logic and morality and induces the reader to think about the Holocaust in an ethically engaged way. By involving the reader, Amis renders the atrocity of the genocide part of our experience as readers and forces us to contemplate "the nature of the offence" (176). This reduces our distance from the event and encourages us to reflect upon our own implication in and complacency toward violence and brutality: *Time's Arrow* has the power to move the reader beyond pathos to feelings of moral responsibility and guilt.

As Alvin Rosenfeld has noted, Holocaust literature has a moral obligation to be "a testament of our times"[350], that is, a medium of cultural memory: *Time's*

---

[350] A. Rosenfeld, *A Double Dying: Reflections on Holocaust Literature*, Bloomington: Indiana University Press, 1980, p. 15.

Arrow fulfils this duty, representing a remarkable contribution to the literary commemoration of the Holocaust. Amis inscribes the moral issue of Holocaust remembrance within a postmodern discourse which focuses on the *stylistic* "nature of the offence" and reproduces it in the form of the novel itself: "The offence was unique, not in its cruelty, not in its cowardice, but in its style – in its combination of the atavistic and the modern. It was, at once, reptilian and 'logistical'" (176).

Accordingly, the time's reversal and the narrator's false perception of reality serve the moral purpose of exposing the topsy-turvy nature of Nazi "rationality", according to which killing the Jews was the means to heal the Aryan race. Through style, Amis has created a *"chronillogical* world"[351] that captures the absurdity of Nazi ideology and exposes the moral reversal at the heart of the Nazi genocidal project:

> By progressing backwards, the narrative style in and of itself comments on the Nazi's paradoxical version of "progress" – that is, the revitalization of archaic myths in the name of national renewal. [...] Nazi "rationality", as Amis points out time and time again, blurred the lines between creation and destruction, as destruction was often rationalized as a means to create. Such "logic" underlies the notion that genocidal mass murder will lead to racial (Aryan) revival as well as the idea that violence is the way to national renewal.[352]

Amis's linguistic and stylistic experiments, mimicking the symptoms of trauma, form a powerful way to deal with traumatic memory. Our efforts to read the backward story frontward perpetuate the trauma and compel us to consider our own position with respect to the Holocaust: as the narrator tries to undo history, our very reading re-does it, perpetuating the atrocities and thus implicating us in the Nazi genocide. Therefore, the experimental quality of the novel does not detract from the authenticity of the horrors it depicts; instead, it is precisely Amis's style that invites readers to sympathetic imagination and critical self-reflection, which are the most ethically appropriate responses to trauma literature. By actively engaging the reader, the time's reversal and the peculiar status of the narrator are the main stylistic elements which allow Amis's novel to convey the unspeakable and unrepresentable nature of the Holocaust: this makes *Time's Arrow* one of the most significant examples of trauma fiction.

---

[351] D. McCarthy, "The Limits of Irony: the Chronillogical World of Martin Amis's *Time's Arrow*", *War, Literature, and the Arts* 11.1 (1999), p. 296.
[352] G. Harris, "Men Giving Birth to New World Orders: Martin Amis's *Time's Arrow*", *Studies in the Novel* 31.4 (1999), p. 489.

BIBLIOGRAPHY

- Trauma Studies and Holocaust Studies

Aberbach, David. *Surviving Trauma: Loss, Literature, and Psychoanalysis*. New Haven, London: Yale University Press, 1989.
Agamben, Giorgio. *Quel che resta di Auschwitz*. Torino: Bollati Boringhieri, 1998.
American Psychiatric Association, *Diagnostic and Statistical Manual of Mental Disorders DSM-III-TR (Text Revision)*, 3rd ed. rev. Washington: American Psychiatric Publishing, 1987.
American Psychiatric Association, *Diagnostic and Statistical Manual of Mental Disorders DSM-IV-TR (Text Revision)*, 4th ed. rev. Washington: American Psychiatric Publishing, 2000.
Arendt, Hannah. *Eichmann in Jerusalem: A Report on the Banality of Evil*. New York: Penguin Books, 1994.
Baer, Ulrich. "To Give Memory a Place: Holocaust Photography and the Landscape Tradition". *Representations* 69 (2000): 38-62.
Baldwin, David, ed. *Trauma Information Pages*. 2005. <http://www.trauma-pages.com>.
Bedard, Michele, Jennifer L. Greif, and Todd C. Buckley. "International Publication Trends in the Traumatic Stress Literature". *Journal of Traumatic Stress* 17.2 (2004): 97–101.
Belau, Linda. "Trauma and the Material Signifier". *Postmodern Culture: An Electronic Journal of Interdisciplinary Criticism* 11.2 (2001). <http://muse.uq.edu.au/journals/pmc/v011/11.2belau.html>.
Berens, Cornelia, ed. *Trauma Research Net: International Network for Interdisciplinary Research about the Impact of Traumatic Experience on the Life of Individuals and Society*. 2005. <http://www.traumaresearch.net>.
Berger, James. "Reviews of: *Representing the Holocaust: History, Theory, Trauma*; *Worlds of Hurt: Reading the Literatures of Trauma*; *Unclaimed Experience: Trauma, Narrative and History*". *Contemporary Literature* 38.3 (1997): 569-83.
Bernard-Donals, Michael. "History and Disaster: Witness, Trauma, and the Problem of Writing the Holocaust". *Clio* 30.2 (2001): 143-168.
Bonomi, Carlo. "Between Symbol and Antisymbol – The Meaning of Trauma Reconsidered". *International Forum of Psychoanalysis* 12.1 (2003): 17-21.
Bonomi, Carlo. "Trauma and the Symbolic Function of the Mind". *International Forum of Psychoanalysis* 13.1-2 (2004): 45-50.
Bracken, Patrick. *Trauma: Culture, Meaning & Philosophy*. London: Whurr Publishers, 2002.
Braun, Robert. "The Holocaust and Problems of Historical Representation". *History and Theory* 33.2 (1994): 172-97.

Caruth, Cathy. "An Interview with G. Hartman". *Studies in romanticism* 35.4 (1996): 631-53.

Caruth, Cathy. "An Interview with Jean Laplanche". *Postmodern Culture: An Electronic Journal of Interdisciplinary Criticism* 11.2 (2001). <http://muse.uq.edu.au/journals/pmc/v011/11.2caruth.html>.

Caruth, Cathy, ed. *Trauma: Explorations in memory*. Baltimore: Johns Hopkins University Press, 1995.

Caruth, Cathy. *Unclaimed Experience: Trauma, Narrative and History*. Baltimore: Johns Hopkins University Press, 1996.

Charcot, Jean-Martin. *Clinical Lectures on Diseases of the Nervous System*. Trans. R. Harris. London: Routledge, 1991.

Celan, Paul. *Selections*. Trans. P. Joris. Berkeley: University of California Press, 2005.

Clark, Mary Marshall. "Resisting Attrition in Stories of Trauma". *Narrative* 13.3 (2005): 294-298.

Claybaugh, Amanda. "The Autobiography of a Substitute: Trauma, History, Howells". *The Yale Journal of Criticism* 18.1 (2005): 45-65.

Crossley, Michele. *Introducing Narrative Psychology: Self, Trauma and the Construction of Meaning*. Buckingham, Philadelphia: Open University Press, 2000.

De Graef, Ortwin, Vivian Liska, and Katrien Vloeberghs. "The Instance of Trauma". *European Journal of English Studies* 7.3 (2003): 247–55.

Dintenfass, Michael. "Truth's Other: Ethics, the History of the Holocaust, and Historiographical Theory after the Linguistic Turn". *History and Theory* 39.1 (2000): 1-20.

Di Prete, Laura. "Don DeLillo's *The Body Artist*: Performing the Body, Narrating Trauma". *Contemporary Literature* 46.3 (2005): 483-510.

Eyerman, Ron. "Cultural Trauma and Collective Memory". *Cultural Trauma. Slavery and the formation of African American Identity*. Cambridge: Cambridge University Press, 2001. 1-22.

Erdle, Birgit. "The Rhetoric of the Void and its Ambiguities". *TRN-Newsletter* 2. Hamburg Institute for Social Research. June 2004. <http://www.traumaresearch.net/focus2/erdle.htm>.

Erichsen, John E. *On Railway and Other Injuries of the Nervous System*. London: Walton & Maberly, 1866.

Erikson, Kai. *Everything in Its Path*. New York: Simon and Schuster, 1976.

Faimon, Mary Beth. "Ties that Bind: Remembering, Mourning, and Healing Historical Trauma". *The American Indian Quarterly* 28.1&2 (2004): 238-251.

Falconer, Rachel. *Hell in Contemporary Literature: Western Descent Narratives Since 1945*. Edinburgh: Edinburgh University Press, 2005.

Farrell, Kirby. *Post-traumatic Culture. Injury and Interpretation in the Nineties*. Baltimore, London: Johns Hopkins University Press, 1998.

Felman, Shoshana. "In an Era of Testimony: Claude Lanzmann's *Shoah*". *Yale French Studies* 97 (2000): 103-150.
Felman, Shoshana, and Laub, Dori. *Testimony: Crises of Witnessing in Literature, Psychoanalysis and History*. New York: Routledge, 1992.
Felman, Shoshana. *The Juridical Unconscious: Trials and Traumas in the Twentieth Century*. Cambridge: Harvard University Press, 2002.
Freud, Sigmund. *Beyond the Pleasure Principle*. London: Norton Library, 1961.
Freud, Sigmund. *Moses and Monotheism*. New York: Vintage Books, 1955.
Friedländer, Saul, ed. *Probing the Limits of Representation: Nazism and the "Final Solution"*. Cambridge, Mass.: Harvard University Press, 1992.
Gross, Andrew, and Michael Hoffman. "Memory, Authority, and Identity: Holocaust Studies in Light of the Wilkomirski Debate". *Biography* 27.1 (2004): 25-47.
Hartman, Geoffrey, ed. *Holocaust Remembrance: The Shapes of Memory*. Oxford, Cambridge: Blackwell, 2002.
Hartman, Geoffrey. "Holocaust Videography, Oral History, and Education". *Tikkun* 16.3 (2001): 51-53.
Hartman, Geoffrey. "On Traumatic Knowledge and Literary Studies". *New Literary History: A Journal of Theory and Interpretation* 26.3 (1995): 537-63.
Hartman, Geoffrey. *Scars of the Spirit: The Struggle Against Inauthenticity*. New York: Palgrave MacMillan, 2002.
Hartman, Geoffrey. *The Longest Shadow: In the Aftermath of the Holocaust*. New York: Palgrave MacMillan, 2002.
Hartman, Geoffrey. "Trauma Within the Limits of Literature". *European Journal of English Studies (EJES)* 7.3 (2003): 257-74.
Hartman, Geoffrey. "Wounded Time: The Holocaust, Jedwabne, and Disaster Writing". *Partisan Review* 69.3 (2002): 367-374.
Herman, Judith Lewis. *Trauma and Recovery: The Aftermath of Violence – from Domestic Abuse to Political Terror*. New York: Basic Books, 1992.
Horowitz, Sara. *Voicing the Void: Muteness and Memory in Holocaust Fiction*. Albany: State University of New York Press, 1997.
Humphrey, Michael. "From Terror to Trauma: Commissioning Truth for National Reconciliation". *Journal for Cultural Research* 6.1 (2000): 7-27.
Ibsch, Elrud, ed. *The Conscience of Humankind: Literature and Traumatic Experiences*. Amsterdam, Atlanta: Rodopi, 2001.
Janet, Pierre M. *Psychological Healing: A Historical and Clinical Study*. New York: Arno Press, 1976.
Kidd, Kenneth B. "'A' is for Auschwitz: Psychoanalysis, Trauma Theory, and the 'Children's Literature of Atrocity'". *Children's Literature* 33 (2005): 120-149.

Kilby, Jane. "The Writing of Trauma: Trauma Theory and the Liberty of Reading". *New Formations: A Journal of Culture/Theory/Politics (NeFo)* 47 (2002): 217-30.

Klemperer, Victor. *I Will Bear Witness: A Diary of the Nazi Years, 1933-1941.* Trans. Martin Chalmers. New York: Random House, 1998.

Klemperer, Victor. *The Language of the Third Reich: LTI – Lingua Tertii Imperii: A Philologist's Notebook.* Trans. M. Brady. London: Athlone Press, 2000.

Kramer, Sven. "Talking around Trauma: on the Relationship between Trauma, Narration and Catharsis in Literature". *TRN-Newsletter 2.* Ham-burg Institute for Social Research. June 2004. <http://www.traumaresearch.net/focus2/kramer.htm>.

Kremer, Lillian. *Holocaust Literature: An Encyclopedia of Writers and their work.* New York: Routledge, 2004.

LaCapra, Dominick. *History and Memory After Auschwitz.* Cornell University Press, 1998.

LaCapra, Dominick. *Representing the Holocaust: History, Theory, Trauma.* Ithaca: Cornell University Press, 1996.

LaCapra, Dominick. "Trauma, Absence, Loss". *Critical Inquiry* 25.4 (1999): 696-727.

LaCapra, Dominick. *Writing History, Writing Trauma.* Baltimore: Johns Hopkins University Press, 2000.

Lang, Berel. *Act and Idea in the Nazi Genocide.* Chicago: University of Chicago Press, 1990.

Lang, Berel. *Holocaust Representation: Art Within the Limits of History and Ethics.* Baltimore, London: Johns Hopkins University Press, 2000.

Lang, Berel. "Is it Possible to Misrepresent the Holocaust?". *History and Theory*, 34.1 (1995): 84-89.

Lang, Berel. *The Future of the Holocaust: Between History and Memory.* New York: Cornell University Press, 1999.

Lang, Berel. *Writing and the Holocaust.* New York, London: Holmes and Meier, 1988.

Langer, Lawrence L. *Admitting the Holocaust: Collected Essays.* New York: Oxford University Press, 1996.

Langer, Lawrence L. *Holocaust Testimonies: The Ruins of Memory.* New Haven, London: Yale University Press, 1991.

Langer, Lawrence L. *The Holocaust and the Literary Imagination.* New Haven, London: Yale University Press, 1977.

Larrabee, Mary J., Stevan Weine, and Alexander P. Woollcott. "*The Wordless Nothing*: Narratives of Trauma and Extremity". *Human Studies* 26 (2003): 353–82.

Laub, Dori, and Nanette Auerhahn. "Knowing and Not Knowing Massive Psychic Trauma: Forms of Traumatic Memory". *International Journal of Psychoanalysis* 74: 287-303.

Levi, Primo. *Survival in Auschwitz: the Nazi Assault on Humanity*. Trans. S. Woolf. New York: Touchstone, 1996. [Trans. from *Se questo è un uomo. La tregua*. Torino: Einaudi, 1989].

Levi, Primo. *The Drowned and the Saved*. Trans. R. Rosenthal. New York: Summit Books, 1988. [Trans. from *I sommersi e i salvati*, Torino: Einaudi, 1986].

Leys, Ruth. *Trauma: A Genealogy*. Chicago: University of Chicago Press, 2000.

Lloyd, David. "Colonial Trauma/Postcolonial Recovery?". *Interventions: International Journal of Postcolonial Studies* 2.2 (2001): 212-28.

Lucas, Brad. "Traumatic Narrative, Narrative Genre, and the Exigencies of Memory". *Utah Foreign Language Review* 9.1 (1999): 30-38.

McRandle, James H. *The Track of the Wolf: Essays on National Socialism and Its Leader, Adolf Hitler*. Evanston: Northwestern University Press, 1965.

Miller, Nancy and Jason Tougaw, eds. *Extremities: Trauma, Testimony and Community*. Urbana: University of Illinois Press, 2002.

Moore, Isabel. "'Speak, You Also': Encircling Trauma". *Journal for Cultural Research* 9.1 (2005): 87-99.

Myers, D. G. "Responsible for Every Single Pain: Holocaust Literature and the Ethics of Interpretation". *Comparative Literature* 51.4 (1999): 266-88.

Oppenheim, Hermann. *Diseases of the Nervous System*. Philadelphia: Lippincott, 1901.

Ragland, Ellie. "The Psychical Nature of Trauma: Freud's Dora, The Young Homosexual Woman, and the *Fort! Da!* Paradigm". *Postmodern Culture: An Electronic Journal of Interdisciplinary Criticism* 11.2 (2001). <http://muse.uq.edu.au/journals/pmc/v011/11.2ragland.html>.

Ramadanovic, Petar. "From Haunting to Trauma: Nietzsche's Active Forgetting and Blanchot's Writing of the Disaster." *Postmodern Culture: An Electronic Journal of Interdisciplinary Criticism* 11.2 (2001). <http://muse.uq.edu.au/journals/pmc/v011/11.2ramadanovic.html>.

Ramadanovic, Petar. "Trauma and Crisis". *Postmodern Culture: An Electronic Journal of Interdisciplinary Criticism* 11.2 (2001). <http://muse.uq.edu.au/journals/pmc/v011/11.2introduction.html>.

Resick Hove, Patricia. *Stress and Trauma*. Hove, East Sussex, UK: Psychology Press, 2001.

Riggs, Thomas, ed. *Reference Guide to Holocaust Literature*. Detroit: St. James Press, 2002.

Robben, Antonius and Marcelo Suárez-Orozco, eds. *Cultures under Siege: Collective Violence and Trauma*. Cambridge: Cambridge University Press, 2000.

Root, Maria. "Reconstructing the Impact of Trauma on Personality". In Brown, Laura, ed. *Personality and Psychopathology: Feminist Reappraisals*. New York: Guilford, 1992, pp. 229-66.

Rosenfeld, Alvin. *A Double Dying: Reflections on Holocaust Literature*. Bloomington: Indiana University Press, 1980.

Rothberg, Michael. *Traumatic Realism: The Demands of Holocaust Representation*. Minneapolis: University of Minnesota Press, 2000.

Rushton, Richard. "The Psychoanalytic Structure of Trauma: *Spellbound*". *Journal for Cultural Research* 8.3 (2004): 371-84.

Segall, Kimberly W. "Stories and Songs in Iraq and South Africa: From Individual Trauma to Collective Mourning Performances". *Comparative Studies of South Asia, Africa and the Middle East* 25.1 (2005): 138-151.

Sebald, Winfrid G. *The Emigrants*. New York: New Directions Publishing Corporation, 1997.

Spiegelman, Art. *Maus: A Survivor's Tale*. New York: Pantheon Books, 1993.

Tal, Kalì. *Worlds of Hurt: Reading the Literatures of Trauma*. Cambridge, New York: Cambridge University Press, 1996.

Toremans, Tom. "Trauma: Theory– Reading (and) Literary Theory in the Wake of Trauma". *European Journal of English Studies* 7.3 (2003): 333–51.

Van der Kolk, Bessel A. "The Body Keeps the Score: Memory and the Evolving Psychobiology of Post Traumatic Stress". *Harvard Review of Psychiatry* 1.5 (1994): 253-265.

Van der Kolk, Bessel A. "Trauma and Memory". In Van der Kolk, Bessel A., ed. *Traumatic Stress: The Effects of Overwhelming Experience on Mind, Body, and Society*. New York: The Guilford Press, 1996, pp. 279-302.

Volkan, Vamik. "Chosen Trauma: Unresolved Mourning". In Volkan, Vamik. *Bloodlines: From Ethnic Pride to Ethnic Terrorism*. Boudler, Colorado: Westview Press, 1998, pp. 36-49.

Whitehead, Anne. "Geoffrey Hartman and the Ethics of Place: Landscape, Memory, Trauma". *European Journal of English Studies* 7.3 (2003): 275–92.

Whitehead, Anne. "The Past as Revenant: Trauma and Haunting in Pat Barker's Another World". *Studies in Contemporary Fiction* 45.2 (2004): 129-46.

Whitehead, Anne. *Trauma Fiction*. Edinburgh: Edinburgh University Press, 2004.

Wiesel, Elie, et al. *Dimensions of the Holocaust*. Evanston: Northwestern University Press, 1977.

Wiesel, Elie. "Why I Write". In Wiesel, Elie. *From the Kingdom of Memory: Reminescences*. New York: Summit Books, 1990, pp. 13-21.

Young, James E. *The Texture of Memory: Holocaust memorials and meaning*. New Haven, London: Yale University Press, 1993.

Young, James E. "Toward a Received History of the Holocaust". *History and Theory* 36.4 (1997): 21-43.

Young, James E. *Writing and Re-Writing the Holocaust: Narrative and the Consequences of Interpretation*. Bloomington: Indiana University Press, 1988.

Zeitlin, Froma I. "The Vicarious Witness: Belated Memory and Authorial Presence in Recent Holocaust Literature", *History and Memory* 10.2 (1998): 5-42.

- By Martin Amis

Amis, Martin. "Buy my Book, Please". *New Yorker* 3 July 1995: 96-99.
Amis, Martin. *Dead Babies*. London: Vintage, 2004.
Amis, Martin. *Experience: A Memoir*. New York: Miramax, 2000.
Amis, Martin. *House of Meetings*. London: Jonathan Cape, 2006.
Amis, Martin. *Koba the Dread: Laughter and the Twenty Million*. London: Vintage, 2003.
Amis, Martin. *London Fields*. London: Vintage, 1999.
Amis, Martin. *Money: A Suicide Note*. London: Vintage, 2005.
Amis, Martin. *The Moronic Inferno*. London: Vintage, 2006.
Amis, Martin. *The Rachel Papers*. New York: Knopf, 1974.
Amis, Martin. *The War against Cliché: Essays and Reviews: 1971-2000*. London: Jonathan Cape, 2001.
Amis, Martin. "Thoroughly Post-Modern Millennium". *The Independent* 8 September 1991: 28.
Amis, Martin. *The Information*. New York: Harper, 1996.
Amis, Martin. *The Rachel Papers*. London: Vintage, 2003.
Amis, Martin. *The War Against Cliché: Essays and Reviews 1971-2000*. London: Vintage, 2002.
Amis, Martin. *Time's Arrow, or the Nature of the Offence*. London: Penguin Books, 1992. [First published by Jonathan Cape, 1991].
Amis, Martin. *Vintage Amis*. London: Vintage, 2004.
Amis, Martin. *Yellow Dog*. London: Vintage, 2004.

- On Martin Amis

Alexander, Victoria. "Martin Amis: Between the Influences of Bellow and Nabokov". *Partisan Review* 1994: 580-90.

Bach, Gerhard. "Memory and Collective Identity: Narrative Strategies against Forgetting". In Berger, Alan, and Gloria Cronin, eds. *Jewish American and Holocaust Literature: Representation in the Postmodern World*. New York: New York State University Press, 2004. 77-91.

Bell, Pearl K. "Fiction Chronicle". *Partisan Review* 59.2 (1992): 282-96.

Bernard, Catherine. "Dismembering/Remembering Mimesis: Martin Amis, Graham Swift". In D'Haen, Theo and Hans Bertens, eds. *British Postmodern Fiction*. Amsterdam: Rodopi, 1993, pp. 121-144.

Brendle, Jeffrey. "Forward to the Past: History and the Reversed Chronology Narrative in Martin Amis's *Time's Arrow*". *The American Journal of Semiotic* 12.1 (1995): 425-445.
Brown, Robert. "Martin Amis: Overview". In Henderson, Lesley, ed. *Contemporary Novelists*. London: St. James's Press, 1991, pp. 36-40.
Buchan, James. "The Return of Dr. Death". *The Spectator* 28 September 1991: 37-8.
Caputo, Nicoletta. "L'etica della forma: strategie di straniamento in *Other People: A Mystery Story* (1981) e *Time's Arrow* (1991) di Martin Amis". *Confronto letterario* 23 (1995): 73-99.
Cory, Mark. "Comedic Distance in Holocaust Literature". *Journal of American Culture* 18.1 (1995): 35-45.
Diedrick, James, ed. *The Martin Amis Web*. 23 Dec 2004. 20 Dec 2005. <http://martinamis.albion.edu>.
Diedrick, James. *Understanding Martin Amis*. Columbia: University of South Carolina Press, 2004.
Easterbrook, Neil. "'I know that it is to do with trash and shit, and that it is wrong in time': Narrative Reversal in Martin Amis's *Time's Arrow*". *Conference of College Teachers of English (CCTE) Studies* 55 (1995): 52-61.
Eddington, Arthur S. *The Nature of the Physical World*, Cambridge: Cambridge University Press, 1928.
Elias, Amy J. "Meta-Mimesis? The Problem of British Postmodern Realism". In D'Haen, Theo and Hans Bertens, eds. *British Postmodern Fiction*. Amsterdam: Rodopi, 1993, pp. 9-31.
Finney, Brian. "What's Amis in Contemporary British Fiction?". 1995. <http://www.csulb.edu/~bhfinney/Amis1.html>.
Harris, Greg. "Men Giving Birth to New World Orders: Martin Amis's *Time's Arrow*". *Studies in the Novel* 31.4 (1999): 489-505.
Henke, Christoph. "Remembering Selves, Constructing Selves. Memory and Identity in Contemporary British Fiction". *Journal for the Study of British Cultures* 10.1 (2003): 77-100.
Joffe, Phil. "Language Damage: Nazis and Naming in Martin Amis's *Time's Arrow*". *Nomina Africana* 9.2 (1995): 1-10.
Lifton, Robert J. *The Nazi Doctors: Medical Killing and the Psychology of Genocide*. New York: Basic Books, 2000.
Marta, Jan. "Postmodernizing the Literature-and-Medicine Canon: Self-Conscious Narration, Unruly Texts, and the *Viae Ruptae* of Narrative Medicine". *Literature and Medicine* 16.1 (1997): 43-69.
Matthews, Sean. "Amis, Martin". *Contemporary Writers in the UK*. British Council - Film and Literature Department. 14 Apr 2006. <http://www.contemporarywriters.com/authors/?p=auth7>.

McCarthy, Dermot. "The Limits of Irony: the Chronillogical World of Martin Amis's *Time's Arrow*". *War, Literature, and the Arts* 11.1 (1999): 294-320.

Menke, Richard. "Narrative Reversal and the Thermodynamics of History in Martin Amis's *Time's Arrow*". *Modern Fiction Studies* 44.4 (1998): 959-80.

Michener, Charles. "Britain's Brat of Letters". *Esquire* 107 (1987): 108-111.

Morse, Donald E. "Overcoming Time: 'The Present of Things Past' in History and Fiction". In Morse, Donald E., ed. *The Delegated Intellect: Emersonian Essays on Literature, Science, and Art in Honor of Don Gifford*. New York: Peter Lang, 1995, pp. 203-23.

Nabokov, Vladimir. *Look at the Harlequins!*. In Nabokov, Vladimir. *Novels 1969-1974*, New York: The Library of America, 1996, pp. 563-747.

Parry, Ann. "The Caesura of the Holocaust in Martin Amis's *Time's Arrow* and Bernhard Schlink's *The Reader*". *Journal of European Studies* 29.3 (1999): 249-60.

Reynolds, Margaret. *Martin Amis: The Essential Guide*. London: Vintage, 2003.

Roessner, Jeffrey. "Unsolving History: The Past as Enigma in Contemporary British Fiction". Ph.D. Dissertation. University of Notre Dame, 1998.

Rosenfeld, Natania. "Turning Back: Retracing Twentieth-Century Trauma in Virginia Wolf, Martin Amis, and W. G. Sebald". *Partial Answers* 2.2 (2004): 109-37.

Slater, Maya. "Problems when Time Moves Backwards: Martin Amis's *Time's Arrow*". *English: The Journal of the English Association* 42.173 (1993): 141-52.

Stokes, Peter. "Martin Amis and the Post-modern Suicide: Tracing the Post-nuclear Narrative at the Fin de Millennium". *Studies in Contemporary Fiction* 38.4 (1997): 300-11.

Thomson, David. "Martin Amis". In *Dictionary of Literary Biography. Volume 194: British Novelists since 1960, Second Series*. Merritt, Moseley, ed. Gale Research, 1998: 7-18.

Tredell, Nicolas, ed. *The Fiction of Martin Amis*. Trumpington: Icon, 2000.

Vice, Sue. "Formal Matters: Martin Amis, *Time's Arrow*". In Vice, Sue. *Holocaust Fiction*. London, New York: Routledge, 2000, pp. 11-37.

Weich, Dave. "Old Martin Amis Is in Your Face Again". *Powell's Author Interviews*. Nov 2003. <http://www.powells.com/authors/ amis.html>.

- **Other references**

Adorno, Theodor. *Aesthetic Theory*. Trans. C. Lenhardt. New York: Routledge, 1984.

Adorno, Theodor. *Prisms*. Trans. Samuel and Shierry Weber. Cambridge, Mass.: MIT Press, 1997.

Ankersmit, Frank R. "Historiography and Postmodernism". *History and Theory* 28.2 (1989): 137-53.

Arnold, Matthew. *Culture and Anarchy*. Cambridge: Cambridge University Press, 1993.

Atkins, Douglas. *Geoffrey Hartman: Criticism as Answerable Style*. London, New York: Routledge, 1990.

Attridge, Derek, Geoff Bennington, and Robert Young, eds. *Post-structuralism and the Question of History*. Cambridge: Cambridge University Press, 1987.

Auerbach, Erich. *Mimesis: The Representation of Reality in Western Literature*. Trans. W. Trask. Princeton: Princeton University Press, 1953.

Barthes, Roland. *Elementi di semiologia*. Torino: Einaudi, 2002.

Barthes, Roland. "The Discourse of History". *Comparative Criticism* 3 (1981): 7-20.

Barthes, Roland. "To Write: An Intransitive Verb?". In Barthes, Roland. *The Rustle of Language*. Trans. R. Howard. Berkley: University of California Press, 1989.

Benjamin, Walter. "Theses on the Philosophy of History". In Benjamin, Walter. *Illuminations*. Trans. H. Zohn. New York: Schocken Books, 1988, pp. 253-264.

Benveniste, Emile. *Problemi di linguistica generale*. Milano: Il Saggiatore, 1990.

Bloom, Harold, et al. *Deconstruction and Criticism*. New York: Seabury Press, 1979.

Burke, Edmund. *A Philosophical Enquiry into the Origins of Our Ideas of the Sublime and the Beautiful*. Oxford: Oxford University Press, 1990.

Carpi, Daniela, et al. *Cultura, scienza, ipertesto*. Trans. D. Carpi. Ravenna: Longo, 1997.

Carpi, Daniela. *In limine: cultura ed enigma*. Firenze: Alinea, 1997.

Carpi, Daniela. *L'ansia della scrittura: parola e silenzio nella narrativa inglese contemporanea*. Napoli: Liguori, 1995.

Carroll, Noel. "Art, Narrative, and Moral Understanding". In Levinson, Jerrold, ed., *Aesthetics and Ethics: Essays at the Intersection*. Cambridge: Cambridge University Press, 1998, pp. 126-160.

Carroll, Noel. "Moderate Moralism". *British Journal of Aesthetics* 36.3 (1996): 223-38.

Conolly, Oliver. Review of *Aesthetics and Ethics: Essays at the Intersection*. *British Journal of Aesthetics* 40.3 (2000): 393-6.

Culler, Jonathan. *On Deconstruction: Theory and Criticism after Structuralism*. London: Routledge, 1983.

Dean, Carolyn J. "Intellectual History and the Prominence of 'Things That Matter". *Rethinking History* 8.4 (2004): 537-47.

De Man, Paul. *The Resistance to Theory*. Minneapolis: University of Minnesota Press, 1986.

Derrida, Jacques. *La scrittura e la differenza*. Torino: Einaudi, 2002.

Derrida, Jacques. *Mal d'archivio: un'impressione freudiana*. Napoli: Filema, 1996.
De Saussure, Ferdinand. *Course in General Linguistics*. Trans. R. Harris. Chicago, Illinois: Open Court, 1986.
Eagleton, Terry. "Capitalism, Modernism and Postmodernism". *New Left Review* 152: 60-73.
Felman, Shoshana, ed. *Literature and Psychoanalysis: the Question of Reading: Otherwise*. Baltimore, London: Johns Hopkins University Press, 1982.
Freud, Sigmund. *Considerazioni attuali sulla guerra e la morte*. Pordenone: Studio Tesi, 1991.
Freud, Sigmund. *The Interpretation of Dreams*. Harmondsworth: Penguin, 1976.
Freud, Sigmund. *The Uncanny*. London: Penguin, 2003.
Fuchs, Eric. "The Mutual Questioning of Ethics and Aesthetics". *Cross Currents* 43.1 (1993): 26-37.
Gąsiorek, Andrzej. *Post-War British Fiction: Realism and After*. London: Edward Arnold, 1995.
Gaut, Berys. "The Ethical Criticism of Art". In Levinson, Jerrold, ed., *Aesthetics and Ethics: Essays at the Intersection*. Cambridge: Cambridge University Press, 1998, pp. 182-203.
Gedi, Noa, and Elam Yigal. "Collective Memory – What is it?". *History and Memory* 8.1 (1996): 30-50.
Gibson, Andrew. *Postmodernity, Ethics and the Novel*. London, New York: Routledge, 1999.
Goethe, Johann Wolfgang. *Faust*. Trans. W. Kaufmann. New York: Anchor, 1990.
Habermas, Jürgen. "Modernity versus Postmodernity". *New German Critique* 22 (1981): 3-14.
Halbwachs, Maurice. *On Collective Memory*, Chicago: University of Chicago Press, 1992.
Harries, Karsten. "The Ethical Significance of Modern Art". *Design for Arts in Education* 89.6 (1988): 2-12.
Hartman, Geoffrey. *Criticism in the Wilderness: the Study of Literature Today*. New Haven, London: Yale University Press, 1980.
Hartman, Geoffrey. *Minor Prophecies: the Literary Essay in the Culture Wars*. Cambridge: Harvard University Press, 1991.
Hartman, Geoffrey. *The Fateful Question of Culture*. New York: Columbia University Press, 1998.
Hartman, Geoffrey, and Daniel O'Hara. *The Geoffrey Hartman Reader*. New York: Fordham University Press, 2004.
Heidegger, Martin. *Introduction to Metaphysics*. Trans. G. Fried and R. Polt. New Haven, London: Yale University Press, 2000.

Heidegger, Martin. *On the Way to Language.* Trans. P. Hertz. New York: Harper, 1982.
Heraclitus, *Fragment 41.*
Hutcheon, Linda. *A Poetics of Postmodernism.* London, New York: Routledge, 1988.
Inglis, Fred. *Cultural Studies.* Oxford, Cambridge: Blackwell, 1993.
Jameson, Fredric. "Postmodernism, Or The Cultural Logic of Late Capitalism", *New Left Review* 146 (1984): 53-92.
Kant, Immanuel. *Critique of Pure Reason.* Trans. P. Guyer and A. Wood. Cambridge: Cambridge University Press, 1998.
Kant, Immanuel. *Critique of the Power of Judgment.* Trans. P. Guyer and A. Wood. Cambridge: Cambridge University Press, 2000.
Knapp, Steven. "Collective Memory and the Actual Past". *Representations* 26 (1989): 123-49.
LaCapra, Dominick. *History and Criticism.* Ithaca, London: Cornell University Press, 1987.
LaCapra, Dominick. *History, Politics, and the Novel.* Ithaca, London: Cornell University Press, 1987.
Leitch, Vincent, et al., eds. *The Norton Anthology of Theory and Criticism.* New York, London: W.W. Norton & Company, 2001.
Longinus. *On the Sublime.* Trans. G.M.A. Grube. Indianapolis: Hackett, 1991.
Lyotard, Jean-François. *The Differend: Phrases in Dispute.* Trans. G. Van Den Abbeele. Minneapolis: University of Columbia Press, 1990.
Lyotard, Jean-François. *The Inhuman: Reflections on Time.* Trans. G. Bennington and R. Bowlby. Oxford, Cambridge: Blackwell, 1993.
Lyotard, Jean-François. *The Postmodern Condition: A Report on Knowledge.* Trans. G. Bennington and B. Massumi. Minneapolis: University of Minnesota Press, 1984.
Lyotard, Jean-François. *The Postmodern Explained.* Trans. J. Pefanis and M. Thomas. Minneapolis: University of Minnesota Press, 1988.
MacIntyre, Alasdair. *After Virtue: A Study in Moral Theory.* New York: Notre Dame University Press, 1981.
Mautner, Thomas, ed. *The Penguin Dictionary of Philosophy*, New York: Penguin Books, 1997.
Miller, Karl. *Doubles: Studies in Literary History.* Oxford: Oxford University Press, 1987.
Munslow, Alun. *Deconstructing History.* London, New York: Routledge, 1997.
Murdoch, Iris. "The Sovereignty of Good Over Other Concepts". In Murdoch, Iris. *Existentialists and Mystics: Writings on Philosophy and Literature.* New York: Penguin Books, 1999, pp. 363-85.
Nora, Pierre. "Between Memory and History: *Les Lieux de Mémoire*". *Representations* 26 (1989): 7-25.

Nora, Pierre. "The Era of Commemoration". In Nora, Pierre. *Realms of memory*. Trans. A. Goldhammer. New York: Columbia University Press, 1998, pp. 609-38.

Oates, Joyce Carol. "Art and Ethics? The (F)Utility of Art". *Salmagundi* 111 (1996): 75-85.

Ricoeur, Paul. *Time and Narrative*. Chicago: Chicago University Press, 1984.

Said, Edward W. "Invention, Memory, and Place". *Critical Inquiry* 26.2 (2000): 175-92.

Sarbin, Theodore. *Narrative Psychology*. New York: Praeger, 1986.

Schama, Simon. *Landscape and Memory*. London: Fontana Press, 1996.

Schwall, Hedwig. "Mind the Gap: Possible Uses of Psychoanalysis in the Study of English Literature. With an Illustration from Joyce's *Eveline*". *European Journal of English Studies* 6.3 (2002): 343-59.

Steiner, George. *Language and Silence: Essays on Language, Literature, and the Inhuman*. New Haven, London: Yale University Press, 1998.

Todorov, Tzvetan. "Poetry and Morality". *Salmagundi* 111 (1996): 69-74.

Varon, Jeremy. "Probing the Limits of the Politics of Representation". *New German Critique* 72 (1997): 83-114.

White, Hayden. *Metahistory: The Historical Imagination in Nineteenth- Century Europe*. Baltimore, London: Johns Hopkins University Press, 1975.

White, Hayden. *Storia e narrazione*. Trans. and ed. D. Carpi. Ravenna: Longo, 1999.

White, Hayden. *The Content of the Form: Narrative Discourse and Historical Representation*. Baltimore: Johns Hopkins University Press, 1987.

White, Hayden. *Tropics of Discourse: Essays in Cultural Criticism*. Baltimore, London: Johns Hopkins University Press, 1985.

ANGLO-AMERIKANISCHE STUDIEN - ANGLO-AMERICAN STUDIES

Herausgegeben von
Rüdiger Ahrens (Würzburg) und Kevin Cope (Baton Rouge)

Band 1 Hedwig Kiesel: Martin Luther - ein Held John Osbornes. *Luther* - Kontext und historischer Hintergrund. 1986.

Band 2 Monika Hoffarth: Martin Luther King und die amerikanische Rassenfrage. Stereotypenkorrektur und humanitäre Erziehung durch literarische Rezeption. 1990.

Band 3 Peter Erlebach / Thomas Michael Stein (eds.): Graham Greene in Perspective. A Critical Symposium. 1992.

Band 4 Kevin L. Cope (Ed.): Compendious Conversations. The Method of Dialogue in the Early Enlightenment. 1992.

Band 5 Zaixin Zhang: Voices of the Self in Daniel Defoe's Fiction. An Alternative Marxist Approach. 1993.

Band 6 Berthold Schoene: The Making of Orcadia. Narrative Identity in the Prose Work of George Mackay Brown. 1995.

Band 7 Wolfgang Gehring: Schülernahe Lebensbereiche in Englischbüchern für die 7. Jahrgangsstufe. Ein Beitrag zur landeskundlichen Lehrwerkkritik. 1996.

Band 8 Klaus Stierstorfer: John Oxenford (1812-1877) as Farceur and Critic of Comedy. 1996.

Band 9 Beth Swan: Fictions of Law. An Investigation of the Law in Eighteenth-Century English Fiction. 1997.

Band 10 Catharina Boerckel: Weibliche Entwicklungsprozesse bei Jane Austen, Elizabeth Gaskell und George Eliot. 1997.

Band 11 Rosamaria Loretelli / Roberto De Romanis (Eds.): Narrating Transgression. Representations of the Criminal in Early Modern England. 1999.

Band 12 Nic Panagopoulos: The Fiction of Joseph Conrad. The Influence of Schopenhauer and Nietzsche. 1998.

Band 13 Roland Kofer: Historische Mehrdimensionalität in den Dramen Christopher Frys. Eine hermeneutische Analyse der thematischen Struktur der einzelnen Dramen. 1999.

Band 14 Anke S. Herling: Phantastische Elemente im postmodernen Roman. Formen und Funktionen non-mimetischer Darstellungsweisen in ausgewählten Werken der englischsprachigen Literatur. 1999.

Band 15 Christian J. Ganter: Hoffnung wider die Hoffnungslosigkeit – Das Irlandbild im Erzählwerk Bernard MacLavertys. Ein imagologischer Beitrag zur englischen Literaturdidaktik. 1999.

Band 16 Claudia Oražem: Political Economy and Fiction in the Early Works of Harriet Martineau. 1999.

Band 17 Kwok-kan Tam / Andrew Parkin / Terry Siu-han Yip (eds.): Shakespeare Global / Local. The Hong Kong Imaginary in Transcultural Production. 2002.

Band 18 Matthias Merkl: Kulturgeographische Inhalte in deutschen Lehrbüchern für den Englischunterricht der 8. Jahrgangsstufe. Ein Beitrag zur landeskundlichen Lehrwerkkritik. 2002.

Band 19 Martina Engel: Außenseiter und Gemeinschaft. Zur Funktion von Interaktion, Kommunikation und sozialem Handeln in den Romanen George Eliots. 2002.

Band 20 Bárbara Arizti: *Textuality as Striptease*: The Discourses of Intimacy in David Lodge's *Changing Places* and *Small World*. 2002.

Band 21 Andrew Parkin: The Rendez-Vous. Poems of Multicultural Experience. 2003.

Band 22 Götz Ahrendt: *For our father's sake, and mother's care*. Zur Eltern-Kind-Beziehung in den Dramen Shakespeares unter Berücksichtigung zeitgenössischer Traktatliteratur und Porträts. 2003.

Band 23 Brian Hooper: Voices in the Heart. Postcolonialism and Identity in Hong Kong Literature. 2003.

Band 24 Alexander Bidell: Das Konzept des Bösen in *Paradise Lost*. Analyse und Interpretation. 2003.

Band 25 Isolde Schmidt: Shakespeare im Leistungskurs Englisch. Eine empirische Untersuchung. 2004.

Band 26 Claudia Schemberg: Achieving 'At-one-ment'. Storytelling and the Concept of the *Self* in Ian McEwan's *The Child in Time, Black Dogs, Enduring Love,* and *Atonement*. 2004.

Band 27 Wing-chi Ki: Jane Austen and the Dialectic of Misrecognition. 2005.

Band 28 Daniela Carpi (ed.): Property Law in Renaissance Literature. 2005.

Band 29 Ina-Patricia Bellinger-Bischoff: Die *New Woman* und das suffragistische Propagandadrama der edwardianischen Zeit. 2005.

Band 30 Sabine Jackson: Robertson Davies and the Quest for a Canadian National Identity. 2006.

Band 31 Sidia Fiorato: The Relationship between Literature and Science in John Banville's Scientific Tetralogy. 2007.

Band 32 Shu-Fang Lai: Charles Reade, George Meredith and Harriet Martineau as Serial Writers of *Once a Week* (1859–1865). 2008.

Band 33 Lyndsay Lunan / Kirsty A. Macdonald / Carla Sassi (eds.): Re-Visioning Scotland. New Readings of the Cultural Canon. 2008.

Band 34 Valentina Adami: Trauma Studies and Literature. Martin Amis's *Time's Arrow* As Trauma Fiction. 2008.

www.peterlang.de

Antje Dallmann / Reinhard Isensee / Philipp Kneis (Eds.)

Picturing America
Trauma, Realism, Politics and Identity in American Visual Culture

Frankfurt am Main, Berlin, Bern, Bruxelles, New York, Oxford, Wien, 2007.
204 S.
ISBN 978-3-631-54940-7 · pb. € 39.–*

The essays collected here reflect upon various aspects of the roles and functions of visual media in (and outside of) contemporary US-American culture. By exercising close readings of the visual cultural texts or of visual media in context, we are presented with examples that illustrate the validity and significance of specific critical theories, while other essays point out ambivalences and subversions in the texts' functions or meanings or present texts that may be regarded as models for diverging conceptual approaches. Amongst the texts discussed are popular television shows like *The West Wing*, *Buffy the Vampire Slayer*, *CSI* and *Nip/Tuck*, films like *The Big Lebowski*, *Bamboozled* and *Traffic*, as well as photographs surrounding 9/11 and questions of identity and globalized culture.

Contents: Picturing Trauma: Professional Photographs of 9/11 as Portraits of Denial; Spirit Photography; The Body Constructing a Narrative · Picturing "Reality": Tracing the Western in *The Big Lebowski*; *Buffy the Vampire Slayer* as Psychotic Narration · Picturing Politics: Three Variations of the Manchurian Candidate; U.S. Entertainment in a Globalizing World; Politics in American Television Shows · Picturing Identity: Depictions of the US-Mexican Border in Film; Depictions of Racism in Spike Lee's *Bamboozled*; Jewish-American Literature and the Question of Food

Frankfurt am Main · Berlin · Bern · Bruxelles · New York · Oxford · Wien
Distribution: Verlag Peter Lang AG
Moosstr. 1, CH-2542 Pieterlen
Telefax 00 41 (0) 32 / 376 17 27

*The €-price includes German tax rate
Prices are subject to change without notice
Homepage http://www.peterlang.de